How To Season And Dry Your Own Wood

How To Season Dry And Your Own Wood

Alan Holtham

GUILD OF MASTER
CRAFTSMAN PUBLICATIONS

First published 2009 by

Guild of Master Craftsman Publications Ltd

166 High Street, Lewes, East Sussex, BN7 1XU

ISBN 978-1-86108-641-9

A catalogue record of this book is available from the
British Library.

Associate Publisher **Jonathan Bailey**
Production Manager **Jim Bulley**
Managing Editor **Gerrie Purcell**
Editor **Beth Wicks**
Managing Art Editor **Gilda Pacitti**
Designer **Chloë Alexander**
Photographer **Alan Holtham**

Colour origination GMC Reprographics
Printed and bound Kyodo National Printing, Thailand

Picture credits
All photographs by Alan Holtham except for:
Page 09 **Bentley Motors**
Page 42 **Woodmizer**
Page 69 **Peter Cox Ltd**
Page 74–77 **Rentokil**
Page 138–141 **Bill Kinsman**
Page 160 **Mark Cass**

Contents

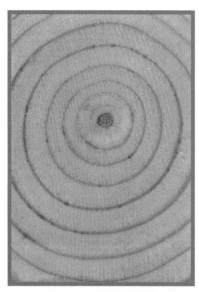

Introduction

"To handle new planed wood, even to look at it is to receive a message that life can still be good at heart; the very shavings are a crisp confirmation, a mystery; it is because wood no matter how chopped, sawn or planed, somehow remains alive. I put my hand on the desk like a hand on a man's shoulder. Into this material has passed rain and sun, it has lived. And some secret part of it still lives. Notice how few men who work with wood are unhappy."

'Delight' by J.B. Priestley

Setting the scene

In this fast changing and frenetic modern world, the tactile quality of wood has a wonderfully calming and comforting influence. Simply sit back and think for a moment about its other remarkable properties. Run your hand over a highly polished piece of decorative timber knowing that for thousands of years man has fashioned this truly universal substance.

Wood is a natural material that has always been present in our lives and, despite all the latest technological advances, is still essential; whether to create high quality car interiors for our highly developed lives or as vital firewood in 'developing' countries. What a comparison of uses for a very exceptional and constant material.

It's exceptional because wood is so unique; no two pieces will ever be the same, even when cut from the same tree. It's also constant because it will always be there; we should never run out of trees as they can be re-grown so quickly. Very quickly in comparison to other natural resources, which can take millions of years. Softwoods in particular can be grown from seed to harvesting within a person's lifetime, a mere blink in the scale of the overall global timetable.

Supply and demand

Yet some 85 per cent of the timber requirements in the UK is imported each year, at an incredible annual cost, to meet our insatiable demand for timber and its associated products. The softwood comes mainly from Scandinavia and the Baltic States, and the hardwoods from Europe, North America and the Tropics.

▼▶ What a comparison of uses for a truly remarkable material.

▶ **Timber can be re-grown relatively quickly.**

Continued clearance of our native broad-leaved woodlands for agriculture, housing, new roads and other developments has exacerbated the problems of shortages at home. The past efforts of the Forestry Authorities and private owners have done little to help. Their legacy is now the massive blocks of well-fenced conifers, grown on a quick rotation for a speedy turnaround of profit, mostly at the expense of generous planting subsidies or tax breaks.

This situation has arisen because most people seem to have disconnected the bond between man and nature. Consequently, they don't take into account the effect this extensive importation of timber has on our own remaining woodlands. Until recently, many of us didn't really care where our wood came from and continued to buy imported timber, often blissfully unaware of the availability of some excellent home-grown material. Without a ready local market, woodland owners had little incentive to manage or to protect their trees, so small estate sawmills closed down and the surrounding woods became derelict.

◀ **Planting initiatives have previously concentrated on quick growing softwoods.**

However, in recent years things appear to be gradually changing. With a much greater interest in sustainability and 'all things natural', manufacturers and woodworkers are beginning to pay more attention to the origin of their raw material, both imported and home-grown.

It isn't just about timber either. Many plants and animals rely on broad-leaved woodlands for survival. The trees also have a major effect on the landscape, often providing an important recreational resource. As well as many other non-timber benefits, such as regulating water flow, air purification and shelter.

A similar situation exists worldwide, although the consequences are much harder to monitor. However, progress is now being made with a host of protection initiatives, such as CITES (Convention on International Trade in Endangered Species of wild flora and fauna) and the FSC (Forest Stewardship Council), making it increasingly difficult to source some of the previously endangered species. These protective measures are making a difference, with many major timber users switching to purchasing wood solely from managed resources.

Trees provide many benefits.

▼ **The FSC is the fastest growing forest certification system.**

Forest Stewardship Council

The FSC is the fastest growing forest certification system in the world. At present there are around 100 million hectares of forest distributed over 79 countries now certified to FSC standards. This represents just 7 per cent of the world's productive forests, so there is still some way to go, even though just under half the companies along the forest product supply chain have already committed to FSC certification.

For us small-scale timber users, this welcomed environmental awareness is something of a double-edged sword. Many of the particularly attractive exotic species are now either no longer available or they're very expensive, leaving us to rely on the less decorative plantation-grown material. Although hopefully this will spur us into more creative design work, to maximize the impact of the available wood. The sacrifice is surely worth a sounder ecological future.

Knowledge

At the workshop level, the more we continue to learn about wood the more it becomes obvious that there's still a lot we don't yet fully understand. This knowledge is constantly being updated. It has already changed dramatically over a relatively short timescale. Even in the late 1800s, no-one really knew much about cellular reproduction, how trees grew or how wood was formed. Now, with the assistance of high-powered microscopes, we can see different types of cells dividing rapidly within the growth tissues. We know that hormones control growth and that these are controlled by both temperature and the length of the day.

A lot of this information is highly scientific and detailed; the problem lies in translating the implications to the average woodworker, so they can understand why a particular piece of wood warps, or why another one is so hard to work with. In fact, how some of the science applies to the reality of utilizing timber is still not fully appreciated.

I was once asked in all seriousness if I got my wood from trees. That may sound like a stupid thing to say, but we often forget that wood is a by-product of trees, primarily formed by the plant to help it to grow and survive, not to produce a workable substance for us. Whatever the final properties of the wood, good or bad, they are determined by the tree from which it came. Wood is not a uniform material like plastic or metal, so to work with it successfully we have to understand the principles of how it grows in the wild.

Why does one oak tree produce timber with very different working characteristics to another only 100 yards away?

The working properties of the wood can be traced back, not just to the tree and its growing conditions, but also to the tree as a living organism made up of many different cells. It's this overall cell structure that determines the characteristics important to us woodworkers, such as machinability, why some woods accept stain better than others, why some bend where others break and why some are more prone to splitting during drying.

The aim of this book is to explore the whole range of functional and physical aspects of wood, and to attempt to explain these using some basic scientific knowledge. I shall look at the structure of wood, showing how the various individual components come together to form features such as reaction wood, burrs, curls and figure.

It's not intended to be a detailed wood science course. Yet no matter how good you are with the tools, some background anatomical knowledge of the raw material is essential so you understand how it all comes about and to minimize the difficulties of working with this wonderful, but often frustrating material.

▶ Even trees growing close together can produce timber with very different working characteristics.

How Wood is Formed

All plants have three main components, roots, stems and leaves. The thing which differentiates trees from other woody plants is their single heavy stem, known as either its trunk or its bole. The trunk provides the bulk of timber used by woodworkers, although other parts of the tree, such as the root, can provide smaller usable pieces often with unusual characteristics.

Divisions of the tree and wood structure

Each of the three parts of the tree has its own unique function. The roots anchor the tree to the ground, taking in water and mineral solutions from the soil. The trunk and the stems take these solutions up to the leaves, as well as providing mechanical support and storage for food materials. The leaves absorb gases from the atmosphere, combining this with water drawn in through the roots, for the miraculous process of photosynthesis which utilizes the sun's energy with chlorophyll as the catalyst. This process turns carbon dioxide into oxygen, as well as producing a sugar solution which is carried in the sap back down the tree to build new cells in the growth areas. This is a very simple explanation of an incredibly complex chemical operation.

Trunk

As it's the stem or trunk which interests us as woodworkers, this is probably the best place to start. The trunk has an outer covering of bark that protects it from temperature changes and mechanical damage. The inner layers of the bark, the phloem, move the food solutions created by the leaves to the areas of growth. As it's rich in these chemical substances, bark is often a good source for extractives such as tannin or dyes. It may also have useful medicinal properties.

Between the bark and the wood is a very thin layer of living cells known as the cambium. This is actively growing material that produces more bark on the outside, as well as new wood towards the inside.

▼ The trunk contains the bulk of the timber used by woodworkers.

▼ Section of a tree trunk showing the various layers.

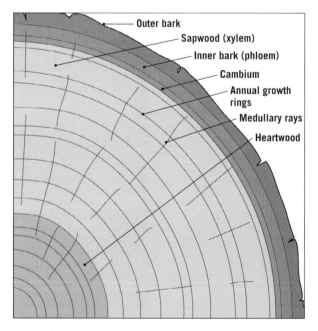

Outer bark
Sapwood (xylem)
Inner bark (phloem)
Cambium
Annual growth rings
Medullary rays
Heartwood

▶ Cut natural edged
bowl blanks during the
winter to retain the bark.

Therefore, wood and bark are only produced when the cambium is growing; which in the case of our temperate regions is during spring and summer.

The cambial cells are very delicate. During the growing season they are also particularly fluid, a feature we woodworkers can exploit. At this time they peel easily and cleanly, leaving a slightly sticky feel to the wood. Throughout the winter, however, the cambial cells become stiffer and stronger and the bark is much more firmly attached. This is all useful information. For instance, if you want to use log cross sections and retain the bark, as in natural edged bowls, cut them during the winter. If you want peeled logs, harvest them in the summer.

Beneath the cambial layer lies the cylinder of wood proper. The most recently formed layers are called the sapwood or xylem. In twigs and small branches, all of this tissue is used to transport sap. Yet as the branch

▶ Extractives deposited
in the heartwood often
produce different colours.

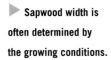

▶ **Sapwood width is often determined by the growing conditions.**

▼ **The central pith.**

gets bigger, less of it is needed for sap. Some of the cells die and the sapwood is transformed into heartwood. This is very significant for woodworkers because the formation of heartwood is characterized by extractives deposited in the cell walls which give the timber many of its characteristics, such as colour and permeability. The distinctive colour associated with decorative woods is entirely due to the deposit of heartwood extractives. These may change the properties of the wood in other ways too, affecting its permeability, increasing the wood's density and therefore its stability, or if abrasive affecting the working properties. For evidence, take a look at some old fence posts. The sapwood usually crumbles away leaving a core of sound heartwood, despite these tissues having the same anatomical structure. It's the addition of the extractives that imparts natural durability.

The sapwood is normally confined to a narrow band between ⅜–2in (1–5cm) wide, and is nearly always a pale cream or yellow colour. Although in some tropical woods the sapwood can be up to 8in (20cm) wide. It also varies among trees of the same age and species depending on their growing conditions. A tree grown in a dense forest with lots of competition for light and water will usually have a smaller sapwood than a faster growing one in a more open location.

At the centre of the trunk is the pith, which may be very distinct as in walnut, or virtually invisible in a timber like boxwood or pink ivory. This pith arrangement is mirrored on a smaller scale as shown in a cross-section of any branch or twig.

Wood structure

Like all living tissues, wood is built from individual building blocks called cells. These vary tremendously in size and shape, with each type adapted for a specific purpose – for example the conduction of water or to provide mechanical strength to the tree. There are two distinct cell systems, one longitudinal up and down the length of the tree and another axial one going across the width of the trunk.

Top prize
The point where the stem anatomy meets the root anatomy is particularly jumbled. This region of the trunk is particularly prized for figured woods and by gunstock makers in particular.

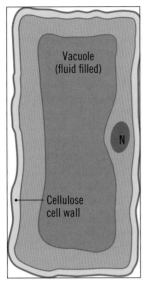

▲ **A generalized plant cell.**

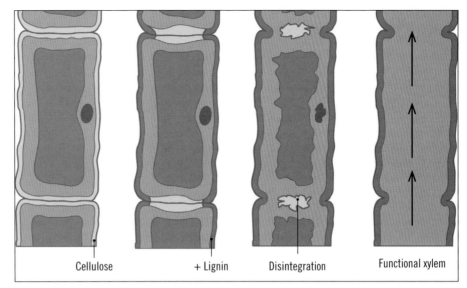

Cellulose   + Lignin   Disintegration   Functional xylem

▲ **Xylem vessel development.**

Wood is made from a particular type of tissue referred to as xylem, essentially dead cells. To understand how xylem forms, it's necessary to first look at the structure of an individual living cell. This consists of a layer of cytoplasm around a central fluid-filled cavity called a vacuole, all contained within a wall of cellulose. Xylem cells are elongated with the long axis orientated parallel to the trunk axis. As it matures, the cytoplasm of xylem cells produces a strong, waterproof substance called lignin. This substance strengthens the cell wall, often creating a variety of unique patterns which can be used to identify the timber at a macro level.

The cytoplasm then dies and, in many cases, the inside cross walls of the cell break down to leave a series of long hollow tubes, referred to as vessels. These vessels conduct water up from the roots and are clearly visible on an end grain section.

Tracheids are smaller xylem cells with distinctly pointed ends, rather than square ones like the vessels. These cells provide the mechanical strength of the resulting timber. It's the way these pointed cells slide past each other during the drying process that largely determine how the timber will 'move'. Tracheids do not permit water to move through them as freely as vessel cells, but they do allow movement sideways or upwards at an angle.

Not all xylem cells die as they mature, some survive to form bands of living tissue spread throughout the xylem. This tissue is called parenchyma and allows movement of materials other than water around the woody tissue. Parenchyma also develops in radial bands known as medullary rays which transport materials across the width of the trunk. Some of these rays will run from the newest xylem layers right through to the pith, while others will be very short. Consequently, the rays may be small and insignificant in species such as beech, or highly visible as in oak or plane, giving these species their highly distinctive figure. The highly nutritious sap needs to be transported downwards from the leaves to the actively growing cambium layer

▽ **The rays may be highly distinctive, as in English oak.**

▲ **Annual rings are highly distinctive in temperate timbers...**

as well as the roots; this occurs in the phloem cells on the outside of the cambium. The phloem cells are very similar to the xylem, but they always maintain their living cytoplasm. Unfortunately, their sugary contents tempt both animals and insects, such as bark beetles.

To minimize this danger, the fragile phloem is protected by the soft, corky, yet waterproof layer of bark made from a tissue called phellem. This protective layer grows constantly to keep up with the expanding trunk and to replace any that's worn away or flakes off. If the phloem is severely damaged all the way around the trunk, the tree is effectively 'ringed'. The roots then become starved of food and can no longer absorb water, so the tree dies.

Annual rings

The cross-section of a tree shows several concentric layers called growth rings. Each ring is the wood produced by the cambial layer in a single growing season. In temperate regions, the yearly cycle of a growing period followed by dormancy results in an annual ring. Yet in tropical climates, as growing seasons

are not so distinctive, the annual ring is less distinct. These rings are distinct because the tissue formed at the beginning of the season is very different to that formed later on; these zones are called earlywood and latewood. The earlywood is usually formed very quickly while the tree is actively growing and calling for fast transportation of sap. The latewood, on the other hand, is stronger and more solid, providing mechanical support to the earlywood. These factors all contribute to the texture of the wood, something we will consider in more detail later.

▶ **... but less so in tropical timbers.**

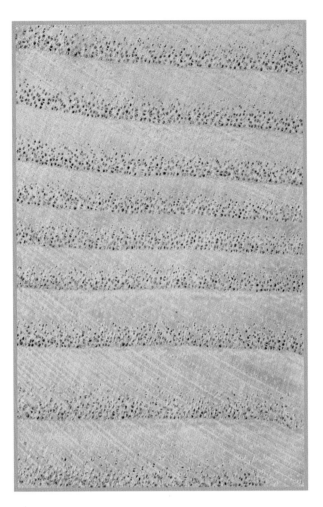

Differences between the earlywood and latewood determine the texture.

Sapwood soon deteriorates if left exposed to the weather.

Growth rings

The pattern of annual rings can sometimes be distorted by interruptions in growth due to fire, drought or defoliation due to insect attack, for instance. How fascinating that natural phenomena occurring many years ago are mirrored in the very timber we're working with today. The science of dendrochronology allows accurate dating of timber by reference to growth ring patterns.

Grain, figure and texture

We also need to define three commonly applied terms: grain, figure and texture. These terms all originate from the way the cell structure is revealed in the finished timber, yet they are often confused.

Grain is the most misused term. People often say 'what a lovely grain', when they actually mean 'what lovely figure'. Grain is a specific technical term referring to the direction of the water-conducting fibres relative to the longitudinal axis of the tree, or the axis of individual pieces of timber. If a piece of timber is split with an axe, the cut usually follows the path of the fibres. However, as most conversion is carried out by sawing, it's rare that the grain ends up truly parallel to an edge. Grain direction becomes important in operations like planing, where it's important to work with the grain to avoid tearing down into the surface. The way the timber surface appears is often down to how it reflects the light, which is largely determined by the grain direction.

There are three main grain types depending on how the log is cut. Quarter sawn grain is produced when a log is cut along its radius and is usually straight and uniform. Tangential grain is created when the cut is made at a tangent to the growth rings to produce flat sawn boards, usually displaying much more pattern.

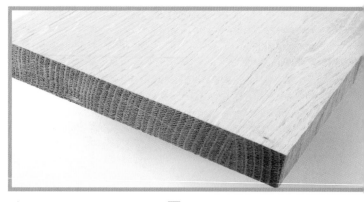

◀ Grain is the direction in which the fibres have been laid down relative to the axis of the board.

Transverse or end grain results from cutting across a log perpendicularly to show the growth rings. However, grain can also be used to describe other features, such as where the earlywood is much more prominent than the latewood, referred to as uneven grained timber. Where there is less contrast the wood is even grained. If the vessels or pores are large the timber is described as coarse grained; if they are small it's referred to as fine grained.

Figure is the pattern produced on the surface of a board by the arrangement of all the different tissues, combined with the nature of the grain. Some timbers have a very uniform cell structure, like beech or

▲ Quarter sawn grain is usually straight and uniform.

▼ Tangential grain produces much more pattern.

▼ Radial and transverse surfaces.

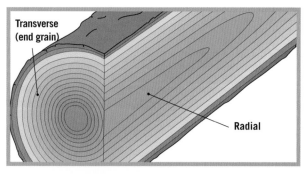

▼ The size of the pores determines the coarseness of the grain.

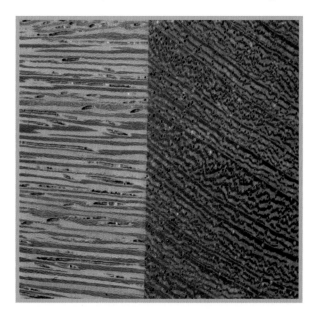

▼ Tangential surfaces.

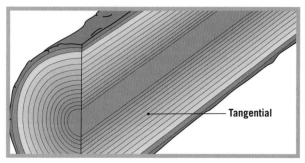

▶ **Complex tissue structures result in decorative figuring.**

jelutong, and therefore exhibit very little in the way of figure. Other species have a much more variable tissue structure, resulting in very decorative figuring.

Texture refers to the size of the cells and the size variation, particularly the distribution and size of the larger hollow vessels. There are several possible texture variations; coarse or fine depending on the size of the cells, even or uneven depending on the cell distribution. As an example, uneven textured species, such as elm or ash, show marked figuring due to the distribution of the earlywood and latewood in the rings. This is where confusion with the term grain occurs.

This is a very simplified look at the anatomy of trees. In reality, the structure is much more complex. Yet this basic introduction goes some way to providing an insight into how the individual cell structure affects the working properties of the resulting timber. Unlike many uniform man-made materials, wood remains orthotropic, its properties inconsistent in all directions. Wood expands and contracts differently in different planes. Its colour and strength properties are also highly variable even within a single piece. Such is the appeal of timber, with its unique and often very frustrating characteristics.

◀ **The contrast in earlywood and latewood affects the texture.**

Timber Classification

To us woodworkers there are basically two types of wood, hardwood and softwood. However, these terms are often loosely applied and it's important to recognize that the classification is botanical not physical.

Classification of trees

Timbers are commonly referred to by their common or commercial names. This is usually sufficient as everybody knows names like oak and pine. It's when trade or vernacular names are used that the situation becomes more confusing. Ironwood is a classic example, with dozens of distinctly different timbers from all over the world referred to as ironwood because of their hardness. Another example is the beautiful Brazilian timber Goncalo alves, which is confusingly known as zebrawood in the UK, but tigerwood in the USA.

These inconsistencies in common names vary from country to country and even within different areas within a country. Fortunately there's a unique botanical classification allowing anyone, anywhere in the world, in any language, to accurately identify a particular timber. The one we use was developed by the Swedish botanist Carl Linnaeus in 1758.

With its Latin and Greek based terminology, this may appear too scientific and therefore possibly irrelevant at the workshop level. Yet a sound grasp of the basic classification is essential for accurate identification of the different species.

▼ *Goncalo alves*, variously called tigerwood or zebrawood.

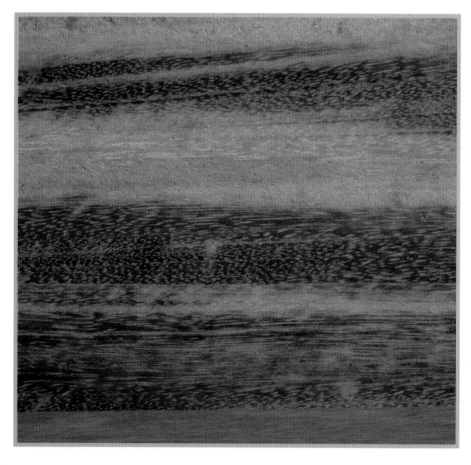

▼ The Linnaean classification system developed in 1758.

▼ **Excurrent form of conifers.**

▷ **Gymnosperms are characterized by needles and bare seeds.**

Every living organism can be placed in either the animal or plant kingdom. Each of these kingdoms are then further subdivided, becoming more and more detailed as you go. The classification is as follows:

Division >subdivision >order >family >genus >species > sub species

Spermatophytes

The plant kingdom has several major divisions, yet the one that interests us is the spermatophytes, which includes all the seed-bearing plants. It's two sub-divisions are based on how seeds are carried on the plant. It's at this stage that we get the botanical difference between softwoods and hardwoods.

Gymnosperms are plants characterized by needle-shaped leaves with cones containing 'naked' seeds, those without an outer covering. This subdivision includes all trees producing softwood timber, all with an excurrent form which means just a single main stem with regular lateral branching, for example, pine and spruce. Nearly all these plants are evergreen with the odd exceptions losing their needles in the autumn, such as larch.

The angiosperms have large distinct leaves and, in the northern hemisphere at least, are mostly deciduous losing their leaves in winter. Some southern hemisphere and tropical hardwoods are evergreen. What all the angiosperms have in common is that their seeds are encased in a cover, either a fleshy fruit or a tough shell such as a nut or acorn. This includes all trees producing hardwood timber.

These sub-divisions are further broken down into orders, two in the case of angiosperms, monocotyledons (monocots) and dicotyledons (dicots). Monocots, such as bamboo, palms and the grasses, have a single seed leaf and are of little interest to us woodworkers. Dicots have two seed leaves and include all deciduous hardwoods. Their form is described as dendritic, a main trunk with irregular branching and re-branching.

▼ **Angiosperms all have their seeds covered by a fruit or a shell.**

23

The next division is into families, four in the case of softwoods, and well over twenty in hardwoods. It's only really from here on in the classification that we are interested as woodworkers.

Further division

When identifying wood it's helpful to know the family, but it's more important to know the genus and species. For example, if we wanted the correct classification for European oak it would be:

Details

Note that the genus always has a capital letter, the species is all lower case and the scientific names should always be italicized. If you just want oak and are not particular about the species, the designation is *Quercus sp.* If there are several species of one genus mixed together the correct labelling is *Quercus spp.*

Kingdom	Division	Subdivision	Order	Family	Genus	Species
Plant	Spermatophyte	Angiosperm	Dicotyledons	Fagaceae	Quercus	robur

In reality, we would ask for *Quercus robur* to ensure that we get European oak. For American red oak, everything would be the same except that the species is *Quercus rubra*.

Be aware that botanical classification can be misleading when you're looking at the working properties. Remember that the terms hardwood and softwood are a scientific classification – gymnosperm or angiosperm, for example, do not refer to the timber's physical hardness. Two classic anomalies are balsa which is classed as a hardwood when in reality it's extremely soft; and yew which is classed as a softwood although it's very hard.

▷ **Dendritic form of deciduous hardwoods.**

Softwoods
Anatomy

The structure of softwood timber is very simple as it's almost entirely made up from one type of cell called tracheids. These are long thin fibre-like cells, varying in length from $^3/_{32} - ^{25}/_{64}$ in (2–10mm), which all come together to form one continuous mass. A closer examination of tracheids reveals that their internal structure varies to suit their specific function. Thin-walled tracheids with large hollow centres distribute sap around the tree, while thick-walled ones provide the mechanical strength to keep the tree upright.

The arrangement of these different cells is not haphazard. Thin-walled cells are laid down early in the growing season when demands for water by emerging leaves is greatest. Later in the year, when growth slows, the requirement is more for mechanical support, so the newly forming tracheids are thick-walled and therefore more rigid. This creates growth rings which are very evident in the end grain surface; one complete ring consists of a zone of thin and thick-walled tracheids.

The quality of the resulting timber depends on the proportion of each of these cells, shown by the difference in ring width in the two samples on page 26. The sample on the left has grown very slowly compared to the one on the right. Generally, the more latewood thick-walled cells the stronger the wood; so the left sample would be denser and stronger.

To complicate matters, the wood in these two zones acts differently when we work with it. How often have you sanded a piece of softwood, only to find the finished surface is very uneven? The thin-walled conducting cells of the earlywood sand

▼ The structure of softwood timber is very simple as it's almost entirely made up from one type of cell called tracheids.

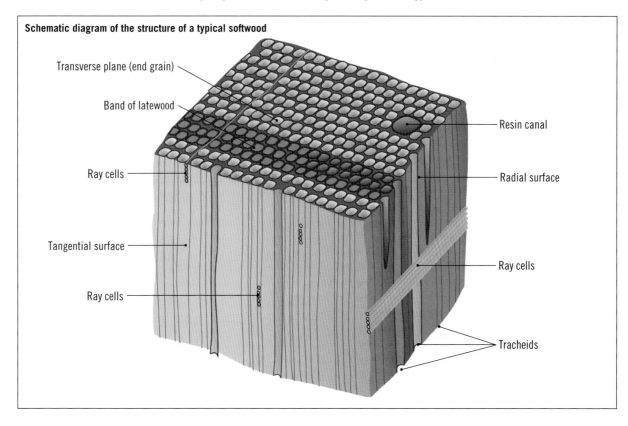

Schematic diagram of the structure of a typical softwood

Transverse plane (end grain)

Band of latewood

Resin canal

Ray cells

Radial surface

Tangential surface

Ray cells

Ray cells

Tracheids

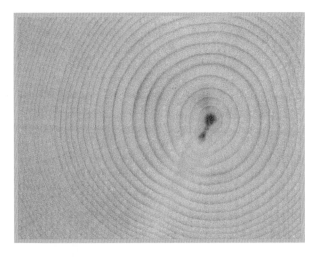

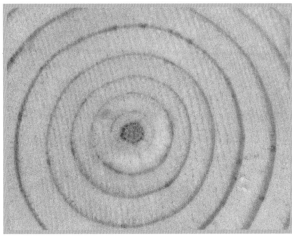

◁ **The width of annual rings is determined by the growth rate.**

△ **There is little appreciable shrinkage or movement with softwoods.**

Growth rate

The top specimen in the growth ring picture above shows how the growth rate has gradually declined over the years. This is usually a sign of plantation-grown material, which starts off with little or no competition. As the tree and those surrounding it grow larger, the canopy closes over and competition for light and air increases causing growth to slowly decline. It's a fascinating snapshot of years gone by. In comparison, a park grown or hedgerow tree will show a very similar growth rate throughout its life.

away much more readily than the stronger-walled latewood cells. On the other hand, the structure of some softwood, like the true yellow pine *Pinus strobus* always used by pattern makers, is much more uniform, consequently it's used where quality and evenness of finish are paramount. As the cells are so uniform, there is also little appreciable shrinkage or movement.

The only other important type of cell in softwoods are ray cells. These are usually clumped together in horizontal bands radiating out from the centre of the tree. Unlike hardwoods where these are clearly visible, the ray cells of softwoods are virtually invisible. Their main function is storage, but due to their sparse distribution they have very little influence on either the decorative or working properties of the timber.

Resin

Another feature of softwoods that is highly relevant to its working properties is resin. Most softwoods are resinous to some extent which is what gives them their distinct smell. Cedar is a good example as the freshly cut timber may feel sticky to the touch. The resin is formed in resin canals, cavities in the wood lined with epithelial cells which exude the resin into the cavity.

◀ **Resin canals often form in softwoods.**

Hardwoods

The anatomy of hardwood species is totally different to that of softwoods. Vessels provide distinct specialized tissues for conduction with the fibres for mechanical support. The presence or absence of vessels is the easiest way to distinguish between hardwoods and softwoods. So next time you are attempting to identify whether an unidentified piece of wood is softwood or hardwood, look for vessels to narrow down your search. The cambial cells of hardwoods also tend to be smaller. It's rare for a mature hardwood cell to be longer than $^3/_{32}$ in (2mm) compared to the $^{25}/_{64}$ in (10mm) of a softwood tracheid.

Vessels are essentially small hollow pipes made from rows of tubular cells end to end. In some woods they may be large enough to be seen with the naked eye. They give the appearance of fine scratches like the vessel lines so characteristic of wenge or porcupine wood. These can be used to dramatic effect in turning.

The presence or absence of resin canals is useful for identifying timber samples. They are always present in species such as larch, pine and spruce, but rarely within the true firs, sequoia or yew. If you expose a resin canal when machining, you can see just how fluid this resin can be, sometimes literally flowing out. It may take years before it solidifies naturally, so kiln schedules for softwoods often include a final high temperature phase to try to set the resin and to prevent bleed problems later on.

Resin pockets can develop as result of injury to the tree, so may form in species which do not normally show them. These traumatic resin canals are distributed in rows parallel to the growth rings, where normally they are scattered uniformly throughout the timber. A tree's ability to form resin as a result of injury can be used to harvest a variety of natural products. Some species are intentionally damaged to stimulate the flow of resin, which is then gathered for the production of substances like pine oil, latex and resin.

▶ **The anatomy of hardwood species is totally different to that of softwoods.**

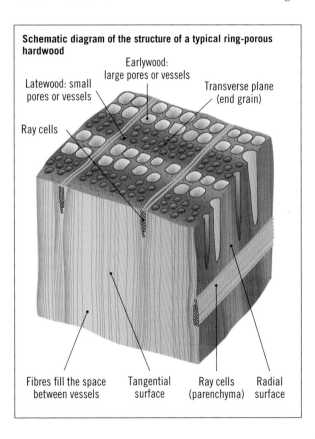

Schematic diagram of the structure of a typical ring-porous hardwood

Earlywood: large pores or vessels

Latewood: small pores or vessels

Transverse plane (end grain)

Ray cells

Fibres fill the space between vessels

Tangential surface

Ray cells (parenchyma)

Radial surface

◁ Vessels appear like
fine scratches in timbers
such as wenge.

▽ The lines are particularly
visible in species such as
porcupine wood.

The vessels are much more efficient at conducting
water up the tree than the equivalent tracheid in
softwood timber. This is necessary when you consider
the very large leaf area of a broad-leaved hardwood
species in comparison to say a softwood conifer with
very small needles. The open nature of vessels can
be demonstrated by blowing down a length of some
hardwoods like a straw.

In a cross-section of a piece of timber, the vessels
can be easily seen distributed either singly or in
clusters, another feature to help identify the species.
Like softwoods, those formed at the beginning of
the season are generally larger and thinner walled
than those formed later on. In some species, those
termed diffuse porous – for example, sycamore –
this variation in size over a year's growth is gradual.
Yet in the ring porous species, the sudden change
in size to the smaller thicker-walled vessels is easily
visible with the naked eye, a classic example of this
is ash. This uneven grain gives the timber a distinct
figure and can make it difficult to stain uniformly
because of the variation in porosity. The distinct wide
areas of vessels are also planes of weakness, so the
timbers are generally easier to split.

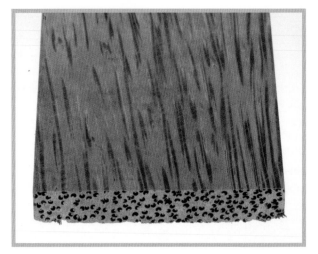

▽ Variation in vessel size is gradual
in diffuse porous timbers like sycamore.

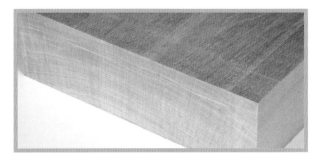

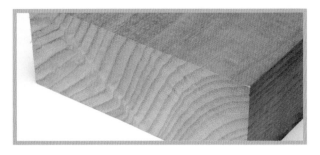

▷ Ring porous species, such as ash,
show wide variation in vessel size.

◤ Blocked vessels on the heartwood causes a distinct line to form between heartwood and softwood.

As the vessels of the sapwood mature into heartwood, they're often blocked by balloon-like structures called tyloses. When all the vessels of the heartwood become blocked, a distinct line forms between the heartwood and the sapwood. In some species, the blockage is gradual with a less distinct differentiation. Tyloses have an important influence on the working properties of wood, affecting the travel of stains and preservatives through certain species for example. Tyloses are also useful for identification purposes, a good example is their absence in the true mahogany family, but their presence in the Philippine mahoganies.

American white oak, for example, is characterized by tyloses in the vessels making it largely impermeable. While American red oak has very few tyloses, the vessels are open from end to end making it very permeable and unsuitable for work such as barrel making. You could therefore easily be caught out just ordering oak or even American oak, it's important to identify the species.

These micro factors determine the more obvious features, such as colour, sapwood and heartwood, texture and figure, all visible with the naked eye and more relevant for determining the suitability of a particular piece of wood.

Rays

Another cell type in hardwoods is fibres, which are shorter and more pointed than vessels. The walls also tend to be much thicker, providing mechanical strength and support to the growing tree. Storage in the hardwood tree occurs in specialized cells called parenchyma. There are many types of parenchyma all with very complicated physiology. The one that is of real interest to us woodworkers is the rays.

Single cell width ray tissue in softwoods is virtually insignificant, yet in hardwoods it can account for up to 20 per cent of the tissue. There is a tremendous

▽ Contrast the ray size and distribution between species such as beech and plane.

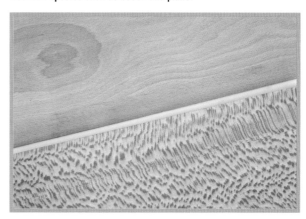

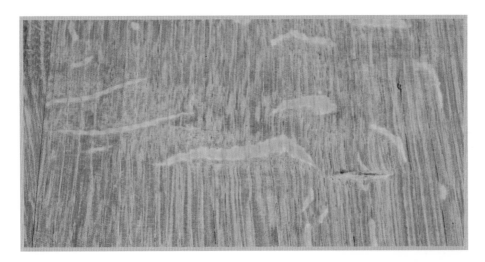

◄ **Rays in oak are highlighted by careful quarter sawing.**

▼ **American oak rays are small and even.**

variation in both the size and the number of rays. In beech, for example, they are small and uniform in size, but in plane they're very wide and conspicuous. Some species, such as oak, have both types, single cell width rays mixed with multi cell width rays, so the large rays are interspersed with fine lines. It's these very broad rays that give the characteristic silver figure of oak, often highlighted by quarter sawing. Contrasting this with the small even rays of the American oak highlights the fact that there is even variation within the same species.

The rays are planes of weakness and often the starting point for the development of drying cracks. They provide natural cleavage planes useful for splitting firewood or for roughing out furniture components.

Although they usually add to the appearance of the timber, it's rare that the plane of the rays exactly coincides with the rest of the timber, so machining heavily figured wood may be more difficult and cause significant tearing.

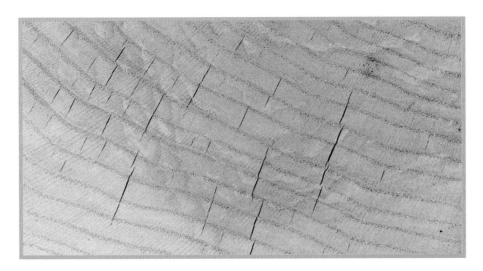

◄ **Drying cracks often develop along the rays.**

◀ Three pieces of plane from the same board, cut with progressive amounts of quartering.

The way the wood is converted can also affect the figure. The picture above shows three pieces of plane from the same board cut with progressive amounts of quartering. The piece cut on the full quarter parallel to the rays, shows much more figure than the piece cut at an angle to the rays which is now just shown as a fleck.

Further properties

The storage tissue may contain crystal deposits of various kinds, either in the rays, the wood itself or both. In ovankol, Brazilian mahogany and purpleheart, these deposits are usually calcium oxalate and are relatively innocuous. Species such as iroko or meranti contain silica deposits which are very abrasive, and therefore affect the working properties of the timber. I have actually drawn sparks when turning a silica encrusted piece of teak.

Unlike softwoods, resin canals rarely occur naturally in hardwoods, with a few exceptions. Normally, gum ducts are found in hardwoods, produced in response to wounding and containing a dark-coloured deposit much more solid than softwood resin. These are characteristic of timbers like zebrano and often occur in response to worm damage.

This illustrates how the microscopic structure of wood results from the demands of the living tree. The type of cell produced, their composition and arrangement, as well as the physical structure all influence the properties of wood. We woodworkers do not need a detailed knowledge of the cell structure of different species. Yet some basic information helps us to understand the simple differences between softwoods and hardwoods and also why different species of the same genus behave differently.

▼ Crystal deposits are a common feature in some tropical hardwoods.

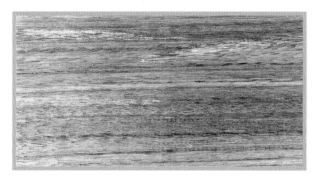

▼ Gum ducts are a result of damage to the tree.

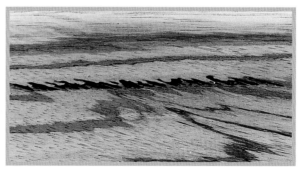

Conversion

When used with reference to sawlogs,
conversion describes the process of cutting
them into usable boards or planks. There is
little scope for using large logs 'in the round',
although some of the traditional woodcrafts
still use smaller section material.

▲ A freshly felled butt is heavy and
unwieldy with relatively little value.

Various options

A freshly felled and trimmed tree trunk is described
as a butt. At this stage it's both heavy and unwieldy.
It has relatively little value and is also difficult to
handle without specialist equipment. Value is only
added when the butt has been converted and dried into
smaller manageable sections.

In most commercial situations, logs are collected
en masse from the forest and taken to a central sawmill
for conversion. However, as timber becomes more
and more scarce, we have seen a growing interest in
converting on site with portable bandsaws or chainsaw
mills. This enables the utilization of individual butts

that were previously inaccessible or not commercially
viable for a sawmill to collect. In the past, much of this
timber was cut for firewood as it's awkward to handle
in one piece without expensive lifting gear. A portable
set-up allows you to turn it into manageable boards on
site, saving on expensive handling costs.

▶ In the forest, logs
are collected en masse.

Pit sawing

Top dog

In the past, butts were converted using a large, two-man saw with the log resting over a sawpit. Obviously, the man standing on top of the log had a much better deal than the one in the bottom of the dark and damp pit, who was continually being showered with wet sawdust. Interestingly, this is where the terms 'top dog' and 'under dog' are thought to have derived from.

Sawmilling

Exactly how sawmilling is done depends on a number of factors including the final use for the timber, the thickness required and the possible figure. It's also important to differentiate between a plank and a board at this stage. A board usually has one or two waney edges, still with bark attached; a plank is more processed with square edges.

Conversion is now carried out on bandmills, essentially large bandsaws with a moving carriage. The log is usually fed past the blade, but on smaller set-ups the log may remain stationary with a saw moving down its length on a rail system. The blade may be mounted horizontally, but on fixed head mills it's mostly mounted vertically.

▲ A board usually has one or two waney edges.

▶ A plank is more processed with two straight edges.

▶ **Conversion is usually carried out on a vertical fixed head mill.**

Circular saws are rarely used for conversion, except in North America where it's traditional to use large circular saws with inserted teeth. These are gradually being replaced with more conventional bandmills that don't generate the same excessive amount of waste.

Methods of converting a butt

The way a log is converted determines how visible the hidden grain features and figure will be in the finished board. It also determines how the timber behaves during drying and subsequent use. Maximizing these features is totally dependant on the skill of the sawyer to assess each individual log for potential figure and cut it accordingly.

There are various ways to cut the log, each producing different effects:

Through and through cutting

This is the most common cutting method in the UK. The cut takes successive tangential slices off the edge of the log and produces maximum yield, although it does little to highlight any figuring from the rays. Through and through sawing is normally reserved for less decorative species, however, it yields a variety of different types of figure depending on exactly where in the log the board comes from.

Each board has two waney edges. The first few boards are crown cut or plain sawn, produced by sawing the log tangentially to the growth rings to create a distinct wide and straight figure. This is the characteristic cut of boards in North American species. Unfortunately, it results in the most unstable boards which will always cup away from the centre.

The next few cuts produce boards with rift figure, which again is straight but narrower than crown cut. There is rarely any evidence of the rays at this stage. As the cuts move nearer to the centre of the log and become increasingly parallel to the rays, varying degrees of figuring start to show, particularly in species such as oak. Consequently, these boards are described as being figure cut. The final cuts towards the centre of the tree are virtually parallel to the rays and produce the most decorative figuring. This is quarter sawn material which is the most highly prized and the most stable.

Cutting a log through and through produces the full range of different figure types, yet there are other methods of conversion that can increase the amount of more desirable rift and quarter sawn material.

Wainscot cut

An initial breaking cut is made down the centre of the log to produce two halves. These are then turned and sawn again with successive cuts at 90° to the breaking cut. This method is normally used for converting species which produce large logs or for oak. Each board has one square edge with growth rings approaching the radial direction more than the tangential, therefore enhancing any ray figure. However, this method tends to be more wasteful as the first crown cuts on either side produce rather narrow boards.

Quarter sawing

To produce true quarter sawn figure in every board, the log is first split into four quarters. Each quarter is then sawn successively on alternate faces so each cut is truly radial. There are two sawing patterns to achieve this. Quarter sawing is very expensive as it produces lots of very narrow boards towards the outer edge of the log. There is also a lot of labour involved turning and realigning the log between each cut.

An alternative is to stand the quartered log section on its apex and cut true radial slices, but this is even more inefficient as it results in lots of waste as many of the boards become feather edged. Timber for making the finest musical instruments is often produced in this way because it minimizes distortion during seasoning or after manufacture and improves the tonal qualities of the wood. This method also maximizes any decorative fiddleback or ray figuring

Methods of conversion

a Through and through giving mostly plain sawn boards

b & **c** Methods for obtaining quarter sawn boards: **b** is true quarter sawn

d Probably the most practical method. Referred to as 'one square edge'. It's produced by cutting the log in half and then tangentially sawing at right angles to the 'breaking cut'.

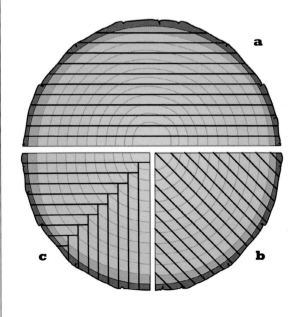

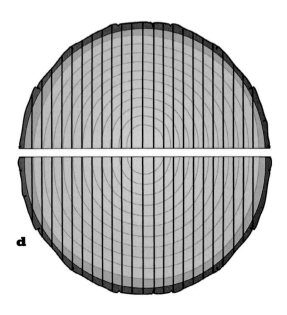

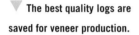

▶ **Logs are marked with a tag, their unique reference.**

▼ **The best quality logs are saved for veneer production.**

The bandmill

To illustrate the conversion process, we will follow the progress of a log through a modern sawmill.

Initial stages

Logs coming into the mill are usually deposited in a holding area for sorting and grading. They are marked with a numbered tag at the point of purchase. These are always either plastic or soft alloy so as not to damage the saw during the cutting process. This is the unique log reference which will follow the timber throughout the process.

A lot of sawlogs are very fluted and often far from straight; this is typical of logs grown in the UK climate. If a really fine specimen occurs, as it occasionally does, these are taken for veneer logs or kept for the highest quality timber production. These are exceptions to the rule, but contrast them with the much larger, straighter and usually perfectly round imported logs. This is purely a reflection of the growing conditions. Tropical logs are produced in a much more favourable climate and soon outgrow competing plants.

Temperate logs on the other hand, have to endure a variety of seasonal weather conditions, as well as competing vegetation, so growth is much more variable. However, these clean straight logs, although efficient to convert, are usually pretty featureless and lacking in the wonderful figure characteristics shown by gnarled and knotty specimens.

Sometimes logs can be covered in small burrs which pose a problem to the timber merchant. Their unevenness on the trunk prevents the logs from sitting squarely on the transport lorry and then the sawtable. These burrs are mostly cut off and discarded at the point of felling to allow the logs to be stacked evenly. The resulting timber, although not highly decorative, has a unique figure. It's referred to as 'pippy' if the burrs are reasonably large, or as 'cats paws' if they're small. The latter are most common on English oak and can sometimes be a real nuisance to the sawmiller. The timber can also be difficult to season because of the mix of densities, frequently with some wood burred and other wood not.

▶ Imported logs are much larger and straighter and usually perfectly round.

▽ Uneven logs with burrs are trimmed at the point of felling.

▲ Moving heavy logs requires an overhead crane or a forklift truck.

▽ Pressure washing is essential to remove grit and soil from the bark.

At the mill

Once a log has been chosen for conversion, it's picked up and moved into the mill using an overhead crane or a lift truck. The use of such heavy tackle is what sets the sawmill apart from the home user. Unconverted tree butts can often weigh several thousand kilos and are impossible to move without proper equipment. Cutting them into smaller pieces, so you can handle them yourself, usually results in so much degrade that it's not worth the effort. Therefore, it's rarely worth the home woodworker attempting to deal with logs in the round; you need heavy lifting gear and a fair degree of experience for it to be possible and safe.

The next stage is very important. The log is pressure washed to remove all the grit and soil that has accumulated on the bark as it's been dragged about. Some mills put the logs through a debarker, which effectively grinds off the bark leaving a neat square section referred to as cant. This works well with straight logs which are fairly uniform in diameter along their length and is ideal for softwoods or plantation grown hardwoods. However, debarkers are rarely used in mills dealing with homegrown hardwoods.

The log is then scanned with a metal detector to locate any buried metal. Both the washing and metal detecting are essential to protect the sawblade.

Hidden metal

Amazingly, anything from nails to horseshoes and even bullets and shrapnel can be found in wood. I once saw part of a metal ladder embedded in the top of one butt! Sawmillers are always suspicious of hedgerow trees as they're likely to have had barbed wire nailed to them.

◁ **Hedgerow trees often contain ingrown metal like barbed wire.**

Just a slight touch on a piece of metal or a small stone can blunt the blade sufficiently for it to start cutting off line. There is then a lot of expensive downtime involved in changing and re-sharpening it, not to mention costs.

Sawing

The clean log is then dropped onto the feed conveyor, controlled by the sawyer. He rolls the log onto the actual saw carriage and positions it precisely using hydraulic rams at the touch of a button. This is essential for the sawyer as minute adjustments to the log's alignment can make significant differences to the outcome.

Most conversion is now carried out on bandmills. These are essentially huge bandsaws, with blades up to 12in (30.5mm) wide and teeth tipped with stellite for prolonging life. The log moves through the saw on a fixed carriage, while the sawyer watches closely for any possible defects. He can control the speed and direction of the carriage, as well as determining the thickness of the board all from his desk console.

If the log is to be sawn through and through it's simply a question of taking off repeated slices at the desired thickness. To cut heavy section material for constructional use, the log is turned for each cut

▶ **The log is then dropped onto the feed conveyor.**

▷ The sawyer controls the log's position with just a button when using hydraulic rams.

▷ Stellite tipped bandsaw blades up to 12in (305mm) wide are used for cutting.

producing large beams. In most mills, the output from the breakdown saw is then split, depending on what is being produced. The main dimension stock then continues down the line for trimming and stacking, but the offcuts are moved sideways onto the resaw line. The main objective is to recover as much as possible from the waste. This is a much more manual process with an operator assessing each piece to determine the most economic size.

The wood moves through the saw on a sliding carriage. This is where it differs the most from the process of converting timber on our domestic bandsaws. Physically pushing a log through a saw is hard work and very difficult to control as it rolls and moves as it goes. The only way to convert small logs safely and accurately at home is to rig up some sort of sliding table which the log can be clamped to.

Even with an efficient resaw line it's amazing just how much is thrown away. It is not uncommon for at least 60 per cent of a log to be lost during conversion into square edged material, although this varies depending on the quality of the log and the dimensions being cut. Nevertheless, a huge pile of firewood soon

▷ Through and through sawing means taking off repeated slices.

Offcuts are resawn to recover some of the waste.

Even with careful recovery, a huge amount of waste material is still generated.

After cutting, the log is re-stacked outside for initial air drying.

develops and can be quite difficult to dispose of. Some of the more modern mills use these offcuts as fuel for heating their kilns. Similarly, vast amounts of wet sawdust present a range of other potential hazards which must be dealt with efficiently.

Once the log has been cut, it's restacked outside for initial air drying with stickers inserted to separate the boards and to allow air circulation. Through and through boards are usually re-formed into the original log shape, while dimension stock is piled into regular stacks with plenty of air circulation. Whatever the method of sticking, there is an unknown cost here for the sawmill. With possibly thousands of logs in stick at any one time, it involves a huge investment in stickers, requiring many hundreds on a busy day, an interesting thought.

All sawn material is air dried for an initial period before kilning. This requires a huge amount of space, hence the need for accurate sticking allowing logs to be stacked to tremendous heights. Heavy section material will obviously need to be kept for a lot longer and soon takes on a beautiful weathered look.

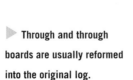

Through and through boards are usually reformed into the original log.

◀ Dimension stock is piled up with plenty of air circulation.

▼ Freshly cut material quickly weathers and discolours on the surface.

Converting on site

It's now more economically viable to convert some logs on site. This turns them into manageable pieces without having to resort to heavy and expensive machinery, therefore reducing transport and handling costs which would otherwise make single log collection uneconomical.

The downside is that such methods are generally slower and relatively more expensive in terms of blade and tooling costs. With chainsaw mills in particular, the waste percentage is also very high, especially when you're producing thin section material.

The mill is guided along a couple of bars fixed onto the log for the initial cut. Once a flat surface has been established, the previous cut surface becomes the guide surface. The big advantage of this system is its ultimate portability. You can transport a chainsaw mill in the back of a car and easily set it up anywhere, even in an inaccessible back garden. Unfortunately, they are noisy, messy and generate lots of waste.

Expense

A chainsaw mill is relatively inexpensive, making it a viable proposition for the home woodworker who uses a lot of material. The biggest expense is the chainsaw itself. The bigger mill models often use two engine units, although for most conversion work a single unit is sufficient. For the more arduous rip cut, it's necessary to fit dedicated cutting chains.

◀ Chainsaw mills are an inexpensive option for converting small logs on site.

▷ **Narrow kerf bandsaw blades generate far less waste than a chainsaw cut.**

▽ **Wood mizer.**

▷ **Small logs can be cut and seasoned by the home user, but often generate lots of waste.**

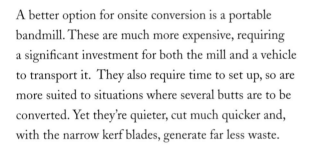

A better option for onsite conversion is a portable bandmill. These are much more expensive, requiring a significant investment for both the mill and a vehicle to transport it. They also require time to set up, so are more suited to situations where several butts are to be converted. Yet they're quieter, cut much quicker and, with the narrow kerf blades, generate far less waste.

Home conversion and seasoning

So, is it possible to cut and season your own wood? In short yes, but there are several big buts to consider. You must be prepared to lose lots of wood and to also put in lots of physically demanding work to get it to a suitable state for drying. The biggest snag is the length of time required. The golden rule of timber taking a year per inch of thickness to dry is not strictly true, but we're still talking years rather than months. It still remains a long-term investment.

The main way to control the use and stability of wood is to remove the large amount of water it contains, this will be covered in detail later. Trying to use wood when it contains this amount of water is simply out of the question, so we have to season it.

The process

The aim is to reduce the moisture level so that it's in balance with the surrounding atmosphere. Yet never forget that wood acts like a sponge; it reabsorbs water as well as giving it up, so the surrounding environment plays a major role in determining the final moisture content. For wood to lose moisture a gradient must be set up through the thickness. As water evaporates from the surface, more is drawn out from the centre to replace it. The faster the surface evaporation occurs, the steeper the gradient needs to be and the faster the drying process. Unfortunately, it's not nearly this simple. Steep moisture gradients induce drying stresses within the timber, resulting in cracking and warping. The drying must be controlled to ensure that there's enough to maintain the gradient, but not enough to cause degrade; a fine balance to maintain. It varies from species to species and also depends on other factors such as thickness and the surrounding humidity. If the gradient is too shallow, the wood may remain wet long enough to be attacked by fungi or other pests. Extra complications are introduced by the physical structure of the wood, the speed and evenness of growth affecting the drying progress and the presence of extractives which are primarily responsible for things like colour. Abnormal tissue, produced by leaning stems or physical damage for instance, also has a direct effect on the way the moisture gradient is established.

All these factors make it very difficult to control the home seasoning process which therefore becomes rather hit and miss, hence the wastage. However, some basic conversion work gives you a greater chance of getting at least something out of your wet logs.

Materials

Large logs take a tremendous amount of handling in the round and are best left to those with suitable equipment. Yet small logs and gardening prunings are well within our scope. Plentiful amounts of free or very cheap wood are available, so it's well worth trying. Although the logs are rarely huge there should

Sources

Local road bypass schemes and garden clearances can yield lots of suitably sized and often free material, but do ask first. This is where you will get the more unusual and valuable timbers from. It's rarely worth bothering with the common species like sycamore or beech, as you can buy these ready seasoned quite cheaply. Instead, look out for less commercial and unusual species, such as hawthorn, yew, holly and fruit woods.

be some useful timber. Having said this, the picture below highlights a couple of problems. Firstly, logs are often cut too small in the mistaken belief that they will be more useful in small pieces. How often have I gone to a felled tree and found it cut into 9in (22.9cm) rings, the usual comment being 'I've cut it into bowl blanks for you!' This totally ruins the timber as we need the grain running the other way to dry it successfully. Secondly, logs in the 6–9in (15.2–22.9cm) diameter range are really neither one thing or another. Of course it depends on what you want to make, but generally these logs are too big to use in the round and too small

◁ **Seasoning logs in the round is difficult, but small ones from garden prunings are worth a try.**

43

▶ **Use the widest possible blade with three or four teeth, making sure it's sharp.**

◀ **Run the log over the planer a few times to create a flat surface.**

◀ **The log is now much more controllable.**

▼ **Round logs are difficult to control by hand.**

to cut into boards. However, woodturners and carvers also require chunky sections, so accept everything. You can throw away anything that doesn't work later.

If you leave these logs in the round they will take forever to dry. They need to be broken down into smaller sections to release moisture and internal growing stresses. If you have a bandsaw with a reasonable depth of cut it's possible to do a small amount of resawing yourself.

Resawing

I use a Startrite 352E bandsaw for the bulk of my cutting. This has a 10in (25.4cm) depth of cut and a sturdy table to take the pounding from these heavy wet logs. Using a coarse blade, something like ⅝in (1.6cm) with a 3 or 4 skip tooth pattern, is ideal, making sure it's sharp. Bi metal blades, despite being slightly more

expensive, will stand up to the process a lot better than conventional blades. The log is often full of abrasive grit and soil, so give it a good hosing with a power washer before cutting it to prevent ruining your blade after only a few inches of cutting.

▲ Screw the log to a homemade jig for a guide.

▶ Small logs are then easy to convert.

▶ Small round logs stored underneath the lathe bench.

To produce a reasonably flat board, the log must be able to slide through the saw easily, which is why sawmills use sliding tables. This is not really possible on small bandsaws as there is no flat surface to slide on, and the log rolls and tips alarmingly. Simply placing the log on the table will demonstrate how tricky the process is going to be.

The easiest solution is to either run it over the planer a few times using the fence for support, or to use a portable hand planer to create the necessary flat. This latter option is probably best as portable planers are usually fitted with TCT blades that don't dull so quickly on the abrasive surface. The resultant flat will provide a much safer and controllable support on the sawtable. You can now gently feed the log through, using the rip fence as a guide if the log is straight, or by eye if not.

Alternatively, make up a sawing jig consisting of two heavy section pieces of timber joined together at right angles. The rough log can then be screwed through the jig at either end to hold it in place as you guide it though the saw, using the rip fence against the back of the jig as a guide.

When you have cut two flat surfaces at 90° to each other you can quickly rip the log through into a series of short boards, revealing the wonder that lies within a seemingly tatty log. Try to keep the heart confined within a single thicker board as this is where all the cracks will develop from. It also offers a chance of getting squares out of the edge material.

Potential problems

Once the log is cut, it's important to imitate sawmill practice. Stack it with stickers between the boards to initiate a drying gradient, and store it carefully. Without doubt the worst enemy is the sun, so keep it protected. Rain is not such a serious problem, but the sudden temperature changes induced by drying it in full sun will quickly reduce the timber to a mass of checks and splits. A steady yet cool air circulation is

▶ **Larger logs need cutting down with a chainsaw first.**

▽ **Never attempt to crosscut logs on the bandsaw.**

▶ **Coating with end seal will minimize splitting.**

▶ **Compare the effects of seasoning with the bark on and off.**

ideal. Initially you can keep it outside, but here in the UK it will not dry to a moisture content of lower than about 15 per cent. It must be brought into a warmer and drier atmosphere for final drying.

If your bandsaw is not upto big sections, rip the log down the centre with a chainsaw first to allow it under the guides. It's amazing just how much material you can cut with this combination of a bandsaw and chainsaw, but be careful. Never attempt to cross cut logs on the bandsaw. This is extremely dangerous, at best you will end up with a buckled blade and pinched fingers as the log is snatched and rolls into the saw.

▽ **Lots of material will be wasted when cutting off the end cracks.**

Smaller branches often pose different problems. Many, like the fruitwoods and ornamental species such as laburnum, are extremely difficult to season in the round. They split badly at the ends and sometimes down their length. This is a shame because they are actually capable of producing some beautiful timber. The only solution is to leave the logs as long as possible, coat them with an end seal of some sort, then stack them away and hope for the best. There are proprietary wax emulsions that can be brushed on to form the seal, but anything like old paint or varnish will slow the drying rate. Even with this precaution, it's amazing how far the end shakes penetrate and how much timber is wasted cutting back to clean material when the log eventually dries. These logs will not be useable for at least two or three years.

Other timbers are more forgiving. I've used yew logs 2–3in (51–76mm) in diameter only 12 months after felling and never encountered any problems. You will gradually build up your own knowledge of which species dry well and how quickly with further experience. Generally, the finer the texture the more difficult it is to dry. Boxwood and lilac are two examples of fine textured woods that are almost impossible to dry in the round without developing longitudinal splits.

The other dilemma is whether or not to leave the bark on. The branches normally split on the end, as the wood dries more quickly through the end relative to the side. If you remove the bark, the moisture gradient across the diameter of the branch becomes too steep, with the outer areas of the branch drying out much quicker than the inner areas. This then causes splits along the length, as well as the ends.

◁ Rough turned bowls should be left thick enough to true up after drying.

▽ Check regularly for insect attack.

Compare the two yew logs in the picture on the left. One log has the bark left on and on the other it has been removed. The longitudinal splits on the debarked logs are deep enough to render it virtually useless, so leave the bark on.

One short cut you can try is to rough turn the timber when it's wet. Getting rid of lots of the waste obviously leaves less material to dry and speeds up the job. You have to leave enough thickness to true up and shape when it has all finally dried, but the drying time of thick bowls can be reduced from several years to just one. Wet wood is also a joy to turn! Even with this method, there will be some failures, especially where the central pith is retained. Sealing some of the exposed end grain areas to try to equalize the speed of drying in different parts of the blank minimizes the problems.

You will have gathered by now that there is no easy answer to the technique of drying your own timber. Providing you always remember the principle of cutting the timber in such a way to maintain an even moisture content across it, you minimize any degrade. You should end up with some very useful timber, but be prepared for lots of disappointments and waste. Hold onto the fact that the results should be worth the wait.

Pests

Be aware that storing lots of wet timber, whether rough turned or as logs, presents an ideal breeding ground for insect pests, so check your stock regularly. Logs with heavy sapwood are particularly vulnerable. Once it becomes reasonably dry, the likelihood of attack is diminished.

▷ Despite seasoning problems, small logs can provide some very useful timber.

Grain and Figure

We've already touched on the expressions grain and figure and how they're easily confused. Things become even more complicated when additional factors, such as texture and lustre, are brought in. Yet it's important to understand the subtle differences between these terms so we can appreciate how the amazingly decorative surface patterns on wood are formed.

Terminology

Grain

Remember that grain refers to the orientation of the fibres relative to the axis of the tree or the edge of a piece of timber. Grain direction is perhaps a better term to use. There are dozens of different phrases that incorporate the word grain, all with specific meanings, yet all referring to either the way the tree has grown or the way it was converted. We talk about working 'with the grain' or 'along the grain' – i.e. parallel to the direction of the fibres. These surfaces then show longitudinal grain or long grain. Cutting perpendicular to the fibre direction results in end grain.

Other terms derive from the position of the growth rings relative to the direction of the cut as well as the appearance this produces. A classic example of this is tangential grain, variously called flat grain, slash grain or plain grain, where the cut is parallel to the growth rings. If the cut surface ends up at right angles to the growth rings it's said to have radial grain. Grain whose orientation varies between these two extremes is referred to as edge grain or quarter grain.

Texture

This refers to the relative size and size variation among the various cells, in particular the vessels. Figure is the distinctive pattern produced on the flat surface of the wood. It results from a combination of the arrangement of the different tissues and the nature of the grain, either as a result of normal growth or from abnormalities. Figure is also determined to a large extent by the orientation of cutting during conversion from the log, as well as the presence of extractives. These have a significant effect on colour properties and can make surface effects even more dramatic.

Lustre

Another property which influences how the overall figure looks is lustre, a measure of how much light is reflected off the surface of the timber. Species which successfully reflect a lot of light off their polished surfaces are said to be lustrous with a definite life and depth to them – for example, satinwood. Highly figured woods have huge variations in the grain angle and distribution which reflects the light in complex patterns and adds modelling to create three-dimensional effects.

Grain types

Put simply, the more uneven the grain and the bigger or more prominent the rays, the more dramatic the figure. If we use the proper meaning of the word figure, several different types of grain can be determined, though they are rarely found in isolation. In pieces with complex figure, two or more grain types are often combined to produce the overall effect.

Let's look at some of the different grain types and their influence on figure.

Straight grain

This is fairly obvious. Straight grain occurs when all the fibres are laid down roughly parallel to the main axis of the tree. Usually, this results in a very bland figure without any distinctive markings. The only redeeming feature is that it's very strong and therefore easy to machine. Any variation from this parallel orientation is termed cross grain which is expressed as grain slope, 1 in 8 or even 1 in 12, for example. This angling results in diagonal grain and, in severe cases, short grain.

▶ Angled grain may be caused by poor cutting

Diagonal grain is not always a natural effect and may be caused by poor orientation of the butt during conversion. What would otherwise be straight grained timber is cut so that the fibres are not running parallel with the axis of the boards, resulting in timber that is weak and difficult to machine.

Even straight grained trees may show localized figure where the grain becomes distorted, for instance where a branch joins the trunk. The log of yew in the picture below is otherwise very plain, the outer surface gives little indication of what lies within, even around the join. However, cutting through the log reveals a wonderful distortion of the grain. Compare the left and right sides of the log; one is straight grained, while the other is very irregular. This is the beginning of the classic crotch figure, formed when a main trunk branches, usually into two equal sizes, as exemplified by mahogany. Yet even within the crotch, there are many variations. A cut through the centre produces the classic feather crotch, but a cut towards the outside of

▶ A rather plain looking log of yew...

▶ ...is cut open to reveal wonderful grain distortion and figure.

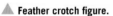
▲ **Feather crotch figure.**

▲ **Swirl figure.**

▼ **Blister figure.**

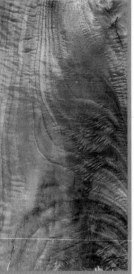

◄ **Quilted figure.**

the crotch produces swirl crotch. An otherwise straight grained tree may also show local distortion at the stump area. The best example is walnut, whose figured timber is highly prized by gunstocks.

Irregular grain

This occurs when the fibre angle varies from the vertical axis in an irregular way. Irregular grain is quite common and leads to the formation of many of the standard figure effects. Although it's attractive, this type of figure can reduce the strength of the timber and may also make it very difficult to machine. Very pronounced round and bulging irregularities in the direction of the grain produce blister figure, shown above in ash. If the irregularities are elongated rather

than round, the resulting figure is quilted. If the grain irregularity is very localized, the figure becomes birds eye. This is thought to be a result of temporary damage to the cambial layer and is most commonly seen in maple. Other combinations of random changes found in grain direction create a wide range of decorative surface patterns, such as the beeswing figure commonly seen in satinwood and the pomelle figure of mahogany.

Spiral grain

This type of grain is formed when the fibres grow in spiral layers as the tree develops, with the spirals being either right or left handed. It should not be confused with diagonal grain. Spiral grain is instantly recognizable on the butt and is characteristic of many fruit trees. The amount of spiral varies at different heights and also has a severe effect on the strength properties of the resulting timber. A grain slope of just 1 in 25, for example, reduces the impact resistance of the timber by 10 per cent.

This is important to bear in mind when you are selecting wood for structural use. It may not be immediately obvious on flat sawn surfaces, but keep a look out for any drying checks as these will usually follow the direction of the grain. Although the exact cause is not known, spiral grain is thought to have a genetic origin.

Pommelle figure.

Birds eye figure.

Interlocked grain

This occurs when the fibres in successive growth layers are laid down in opposite directions. The resulting ribbon or striped figure shows up especially well on quarter sawn pieces. It's quite rare in home-grown timbers, but much more common in many of the tropical imported timbers such as African walnut or sapele. The resulting timber is very difficult to machine and picks up or tears regardless of the way in which you plane it, although the strength properties are rarely affected.

Wavy grain

The feature we're perhaps most familiar with is wavy grain. This occurs where the angle of the fibres is constantly changing, but in a more regular pattern than in irregular grain. To maximize this effect, the timber has to be cut radially, a characteristic of maple and sycamore. The classic example is fiddleback figure. Its wavy grain causes variations in the way light is reflected from the surface, creating a series of lighter and darker stripes.

As the name suggests, this particularly decorative figure is much in demand for the back of stringed musical instruments. It sometimes occurs combined with interlocked grain that breaks up the ripple to

An example of spiral grain.

Spiral grain is easily recognizable on this pear tree.

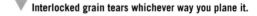
Interlocked grain tears whichever way you plane it.

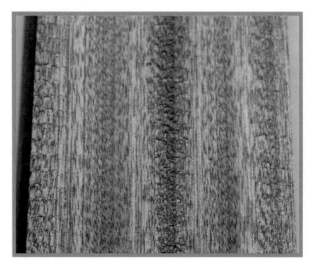

Roe figure.

Fiddleback figure.

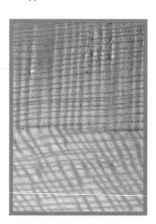

A good example of rippled ash.

Ripple undulations visible under the bark.

produce a figure called roe. As this type of grain is so wavy, you can often spot it even where the surface is very rough or covered in dirt. Ripple figure is a tighter version of fiddleback and is commonly found in sycamore and ash.

Although its exact cause is unknown, it's thought to have something to do with the wind rocking the tree. A good diagnostic aid for ripple is to run your hand down the surface of the trunk after the bark has been stripped off while feeling for the characteristic regular undulations.

Burrs

The term burrs refers to the bulging lumps growing on the outside of the trunk. These often result from some sort of parasitic attack causing a mass of small shoots to grow out of a small area. The resulting timber is a jumble of all the different grain orientations already

Typical oak burr.

Elm burr sliced through.

Richly patterned amboyna burr.

▼ Huge colour variations
exhibited by stripey ebony.

▼ Pigment figure
in goncalo alves.

▼ Silver figure in oak.

▼ Fleck figure in
ropala lacewood.

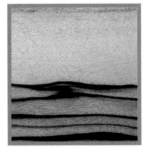

described and yields wonderfully decorative timber. This may vary from open irregular figure, like the piece of elm burr shown below left, through to a more regular closely packed pattern, as in amboyna. As the grain is so jumbled, the resulting timber is very difficult to season and distorts severely as it dries, even when it's in veneer form.

▲ A wonderful combination of different figure types.

Further sources

Figure is not always dependent on grain, but can be determined by other factors such as colour; the term 'pigment figure' covers this. These highly decorative colourations are caused by extractives laid down in an irregular manner in the heartwood. A superb example is stripey ebony. The picture above shows two boards of goncalo alves, both with ripple figure, yet one also has much more pigment figure. The cause of this incredible variation between trees of the same species is again not fully understood. Most likely, it's a combination of genetic features and growing conditions.

Another source of figure is the varying distribution of other growing tissues. The distinctive pattern of silver figure in oak is a result of sawing at 90° to the growth rings to reveal the broad rays. To make this figure more attractive, try reducing the size of the rays by cutting slightly off the true quarter to produce fleck figure, as shown in the piece of ropala lacewood above.

Figure effects are also occasionally caused by insect infestation, as in the case of masur birch where tiny fly larvae burrow into the surface of the timber. The result

is tiny dark brown or black lines of varying direction. We have seen that the presence of a particular grain type is not always enough on its own to produce the desired figure. Careful cutting during conversion is essential to maximize the effects. Often the most dramatic effects are a combination of several types of figure. The picture above shows a piece of ash with ripple, curl, roe and pigment figure, along with a bit of rot and spalting for good measure; this should make an interesting bowl!

▶ Insect
attacks can cause
distinctive patterns
in masur birch.

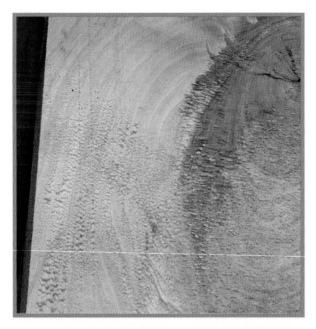

 **Fuzzy grain in reaction wood.**

Texture

As with grain, there are a range of adjectives associated with texture, in particular coarse, fine, even and uneven. The difference between coarse and fine texture depends on the size of the vessels, plus the quantity and size of the rays. Timbers such as oak are coarse textured, the vessels are large and the rays are broad. Where the vessels are small and the rays are narrow, the timber is referred to as fine textured or very fine, as in boxwood. There is obviously a full range of grades in between. The texture may also vary from log to log within the same species. Texture is the term most often confused with grain. Oak for example, is regularly described as open grained, when strictly it should be referred to as coarse textured.

As they lack vessels and the cells are all small in diameter, softwoods are technically fine textured. However, variations in the tracheids' size and growth ring dimensions may result in a rougher machined surface in some species, although this rarely exceeds anything other than moderate texture. Very slow grown high-altitude spruces are specifically chosen for making musical instruments because of their extremely fine texture.

▲ **Fine textured boxwood.**

▼ **High altitude softwoods have a very fine texture.**

Knowing the grain orientation is vital when you come to chisel or plane the wood. Any cut will try to follow the direction of the fibres and split ahead of the cutter. This will not cause problems if the fibres are angled up and away from the edge, but if they're angled downwards into the surface, they tend to tear out to a considerable depth. Therefore, we want to work 'with the grain' rather than 'against the grain' where possible to prevent tear-out. Hardwoods which incorporate areas of reaction wood or juvenile wood, described in more detail later on, are very difficult to cut cleanly in any direction. The rather woolly surface that results is referred to as fuzzy grain.

Even texture in beech.

Uneven texture
characterized by ash.

The contrast between earlywood and latewood
determines the evenness of the texture. Where the
contrast is distinct as in ash, the timber is uneven
textured. Yet where there is little variation, it's termed
even textured, as in sycamore. As before, there is a
whole gradation of textures between the two extremes.

So putting the two components of texture together,
hardwoods can be fine and even textured, for instance
beech. They can also be coarse and even textured as
with many tropical timbers such as iroko or wenge.
Many temperate hardwoods are coarse and uneven
textured, like elm, but this can also apply to tropical
hardwoods such as teak.

Even textured timber often lacks distinct figuring.
Yet this may be an advantage as its very evenness
makes it ideal for uses such as carving where you're
looking to create fine detail. Species like lime or
jelutong are classic carving woods for this very reason.

Fine and even
texture in sycamore.

Coarse and even
texture in wenge.

Even textured species
like lime are ideal for carving.

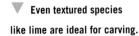

Colour

So far we've looked at the features that make up grain, figure and texture, their origin and their effect on the appearance of wood. Yet one of the most important characteristics is colour as this has the most immediate effect on us and largely determines the decorative value of the timber. Colour, or possibly the lack of it, enhances all the other effects we've covered.

Fuming timber

The colours in a piece of timber are almost entirely due to certain chemicals in the cell walls of the heartwood. We tend to think of lignin and cellulose as the main constituents of wood, but the tree synthesises many other substances. These chemicals are usually all referred to as 'extractives', as most of them can be removed using a range of solvents. The various groups of extractives interact with each other, to a large extent determining the working properties of the timber, and affecting factors such as durability and toxicity.

For now, we only need to concern ourselves with the group of compounds called tannins and their close relatives, the anthocyanins. Some tannins are pigments in their own right; others are totally colourless, but will become coloured when they're mixed with other substances. The prime example is oak and iron. Here the tannin reacts with the metal to form a dark stain in moist conditions. Such is its strength, that the tannin quickly corrodes any steel tools left in contact with the timber. To avoid discolouration, brass fittings and screws are always recommended when using oak. Fuming oak with ammonia to give it a dark rich brown colour is another tannin effect.

How to

Fuming is a very simple technique used to darken timbers which contain tannic acid. Oak is frequently the usual candidate, but chestnut and walnut can also be darkened successfully. As the process involves a chemical reaction within the timber, rather than simply a surface coating, the finished effect is much more even and mimics the appearance of timber darkened naturally through ageing.

◄ **Colour is the most important characteristic of figure.**

Tannins react with metal in moist conditions and stain the timber.

It's better to fume the finished piece as a whole rather than the raw timber. First remove any metal fittings to avoid black stains in the surrounding timber. You will also need to construct a temporary fume tent. This only needs to be a simple framework of softwood offcuts nailed and glued together, then covered in thick gauge black plastic. Damp-proofing membrane obtained from a builder's merchant is ideal as it's cheap and also very strong. The plastic must be black to exclude light and any unwanted variations in colour caused by daylight. It must also be as airtight as possible.

Ammonia is used as the fuming agent. You can usually order this through your local pharmacy. It needs to be a strong solution, ideally 'eighty:eighty ammonia', a 26 per cent solution. Household ammonia will suffice, but the process will be much slower.

Take care when handling ammonia, as the fumes are extremely unpleasant and irritating. Read all the warning sheets carefully and wear suitable safety gear and protective clothing. As an added precaution, I do all my fuming outside, so there's plenty of air circulation. Don't attempt to fume in a confined space.

The fuming tent needs to be covered in black plastic.

Eighty:eighty ammonia works quickly.

Samples enclosed in the tent with two jars of ammonia.

the wood, the darker its colour will be. There are no rules here, just keep checking its progress. With ammonia of this strength, 24 hours in the tent is enough to give a warm, medium dark colour.

Remember that as this is a chemical reaction, the process will continue for some time after the wood is removed from the fumes and the wood will therefore continue to darken. So if the final colour is critical, you need to anticipate the speed of change and take the wood out in good time.

The colouration is only relatively shallow and a pass over the planer with a $5/64$in (2mm) cut will remove the bulk of it. Any cracks or splits in the end grain areas are obviously more porous, so the staining is consequently much deeper.

The procedure

The workpieces are placed inside the tent along with at least two jars of ammonia to generate plenty of fumes. Glass or ceramic jars or dishes should always be used, never metal. Seal the tent opening thoroughly with tape, then leave it to fume. The longer you leave

24 hours in the tent results in a rich dark colouration.

◀ **Staining is much deeper around any cracks and on the end grain.**

▶ **Metal in yew results in deep purple colouration.**

Colouration

Yew is another timber that discolours dramatically, but only when it grows in close contact with metal. Rich purple-coloured veins in the timber are a sure indication that there is metal in there somewhere, usually in the form of nails or wire.

Most timbers can also be lightened using chemical methods. Wood bleaches based on hydrogen peroxide are capable of removing even very dark colours.

However, the bright colours in timber are not always what they first appear to be. The rich red of padauk slowly changes to a dark brown and then an

▼ **Logwood sample recovered from a 300-year-old submerged wreck.**

From the deep

The natural colours of the wood are sometimes exploited to make dyes. Brazilian logwood is a excellent example, whose shavings have been used for centuries to produce a rich yellow textile dye. Logwood therefore, has always been regarded as an extremely precious commodity. Trading ships carrying it were often accompanied by naval escorts as this valuable cargo was a prime target for pirates. I actually have some samples of logwood recovered from a wreck off the North Wales coast, estimated to have been underwater for 200–300 years!

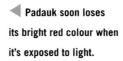

Padauk soon loses its bright red colour when it's exposed to light.

Tulipwood also fades from its initial bright colouration.

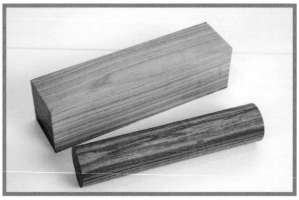

After machining, purpleheart is a grey colour, yet it will gradually regain its purple colouration.

almost black colour. Brazilian tulipwood on the other hand, fades from its purple striped brilliance to a very pale yellow colour. These natural colour changes result from exposure to light, heat or air. They may be very slow as in the case of the padauk, or rapid as in species like purpleheart. In the latter example, freshly planed timber is a very disappointing dull brown colour, yet after a few hours in bright light soon restores its brilliant purple hue.

Sometimes the colour change results from some form of mechanical damage to the tree, affecting the density of the wood. The pale Zimbabwean ebony below shows dark black colouration around

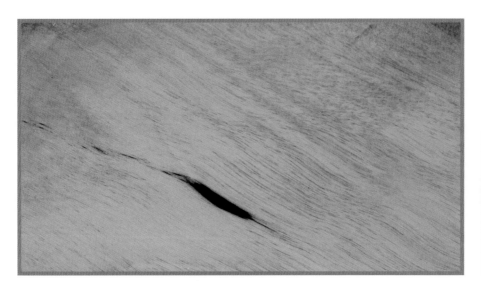

Colour change as the result of worm damage.

Scar tissue in sycamore often has grey/green colouration.

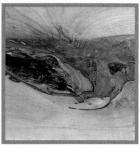

Olive ash results from brown colouration in older logs.

Brown oak is caused by the initial stages of a wood rotting fungal infection.

the wormholes, but rarely anywhere else. Damaged sycamore often produces a dark grey scar tissue, which is much harder to work than the surrounding wood. It would be interesting to know just what material is deposited to produce such a difference in density.

It's thought that the growing conditions, in particular the soil, may also have an effect on the colour of the heartwood. Old ash trees often exhibit the characteristic olive figure, a mass of rich brown hues. Yet a similar tree grown on soil with different acidity shows a distinct green hue. Like sycamore, this colour change is often associated with a change in wood density.

Colour changes in wood that is beginning to decay, may or may not be to our advantage. Brown oak for example, is not a different species, merely ordinary oak infected with *Fistulina hepatica* fungus during the latter stages of growth. The result becomes a gorgeous brown colouration of the heartwood with really distinct golden rays. Unfortunately, if this rotting fungus goes too far, the resulting timber is crumbly and useless with all its mechanical strength destroyed, so it's important that logs are carefully selected.

Other fungal infections can cause colour changes. The classic example of this is spalted beech, which we will cover in more detail in a later chapter. Spalting is caused by a complex interaction of several different fungi. Some advance through the wood in distinct areas, clearly differentiated by dark black zone lines. Behind these come different fungi, some of which feed on the wood by producing enzymes to dissolve lignin and therefore dramatically altering the strength. These are usually associated with a colour change towards yellow, which we would normally recognize as the first stages of rot.

Exposure to light

To complicate matters, some timbers will both fade and darken depending on the intensity of the light. The top of an antique mahogany table left in the direct light of a sunny window usually turns a pale straw colour. While the undercarriage, which has only been exposed to moderate light, remains a dark brown.

To appreciate what is causing these many colour changes, remember that light is a form of radiant energy with a variety of different wavelengths.

Colour differences inside and outside a turned laburnum vase, illustrating the effects of light exposure.

Spalting is another fungal infection effect.

Most of the effects are caused by visible light and the wavelengths around it, ultraviolet and infrared. These have relatively high energy levels and react with the oxygen in the timber to cause chemical reactions that change the natural colour of the wood. Light may also fade applied stains or affect finishes.

The chemistry of this colour change is relatively complicated. You can modify the effects by applying different finishes, but realistically you only stall the process. There is nothing that will prevent natural colour change, other than controlling the amount of strong light. The picture on page 61 shows a laburnum vase turned some 20 years ago. The outside is a rich brown colour, but the inside, which rarely sees the light of day, is still the same golden colour it was when it was first turned. The same effect is visible in very old furniture, often hundreds of years old, where for instance the inside of a door is a completely different colour to the outside. This confirms that it's the effect of light that causes these colour changes.

Direct effects

There are ways this colour change can be used to our advantage and brought about much quicker. Kiln drying produces high temperatures and high humidity, a combination that will darken most timbers to some extent. With careful control this process can be maximized and the colour of timbers, such as beech

and pear, altered considerably. Both turn a distinct pink colour and are consequently known as 'steamed pear' or 'steamed beech'.

Most of the colour effects benefit us woodworkers, further enhancing the overall appearance of the timber. Although, sometimes the colour change is not desirable. Fungi, for example, tends to disfigure and discolour wood rather than adding any decorative value.

Sycamore needs to be end reared to prevent staining.

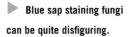

When seasoned incorrectly, sycamore can become stained to a considerable depth.

Blue sap staining fungi can be quite disfiguring.

For instance, sycamore is only regarded as 'prime' quality if it's pure snowy white, but it's quite a tricky species to season. If it's not stored properly, sycamore soon becomes infected with sap staining fungi, resulting in a dirty green discolouration. This may not become immediately obvious by looking at the surface of the timber, but a light pass over the planer soon reveals the colour beneath.

To minimize the risk of discolouration, sycamore is always cut in the winter and then 'end reared' for seasoning. Softwoods may also be infected with a penetrating blue stain fungi, although this is usually confined to the sapwood. Unlike the rotting fungi, sap stain fungi rarely has any effect on the strength of the wood, tending to disfigure it instead and therefore detract from its decorative value.

Another cause of colour change is weathering. If freshly cut timber of any species is left outside without surface treatment, it always turns a very pleasant silvery grey. This is caused by a chemical degradation of the surface, mainly influenced by exposure to ultra violet light. The grey layer is very thin, so even light cutting with a plane will reveal the real colour below, usually a magical transformation.

The final colour is further enhanced by the natural property of lustre, as seen in the previous chapter. This is dependant on the ability of the cell walls to reflect light and is much more distinct in woods like satinwood, which have an undeniable 'life'. The effect of lustre is more pronounced on quarter-sawn surfaces, the colour appearing completely different depending on how the timber is orientated to the light.

When exposed to the weather wood turns grey on the surface.

Fungi and Insects

Although it's theoretically a biodegradable substance, wood will last almost indefinitely, provided it's kept in the right conditions. Yet the inbuilt ability of wood to decay and to return back to the soil is always there, in a state of suspended animation. It's held at bay by man's control, only requiring minor changes in environmental conditions to trigger it off. However, we can delay this inevitable process, primarily by ensuring that the wood is properly dried during seasoning. Left in the wild, trees age and die, then either rot standing up or fall over, returning nutrients to the soil and beginning the growth process once again.

Fungi

Degrade can be brought about by a number of agencies, such as bacteria, insects, borers and fungi. Often there's an interaction between several of these factors, making it difficult to identify the cause and the effect.

Within natural forests, there's a constant supply of dead and dying trees, providing a rich source for fungal infection and growth. Fungi are unable to produce food for themselves. In order to survive they take nourishment from the timber they've infected. The degree to which this affects the timber gives the broad classification of the huge fungal group into moulds, stains and rots.

Moulds and stains

Moulds are infections of the surface, while stains penetrate deeper into the actual cell structure. Both feed off the carbohydrates stored in the cell

Natural forests contain dead and dying trees.

▼ **Moulds are infections on the surface of the timber.**   ▶ **Stains penetrate more deeply.**

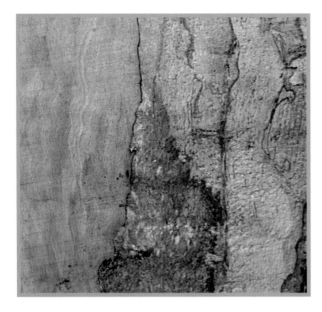

cavities, yet without affecting the cell structure. The most obvious symptom is discolouration, usually an unattractive bluey grey colour. As this is so often confined to the sapwood, these are commonly referred to as sap stain fungi.

Rots

On the other hand, rots are far more destructive. These feed by producing enzymes to break down the cell structure. In the early stages of attack, the so-called incipient decay stage, the first symptom is some form of staining. This is often referred to as 'dote', and initially only moderately affects the strength properties of the timber. However, the decay process is progressive; advanced decay results in a softening of the wood and eventually a total loss of strength.

▼ **Dote or incipient decay.**

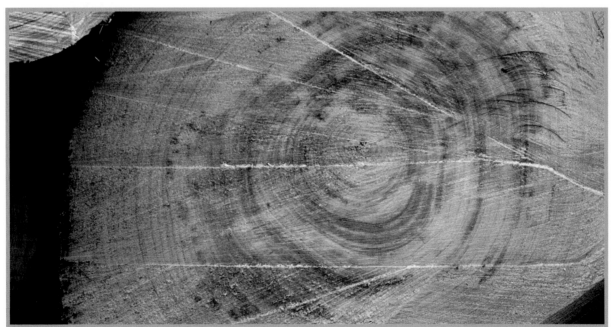

◀ Some fungi will
only rot the heartwood
resulting in hollow trees.

▶ Other fungi only
colonise logs after felling.

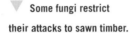

▼ Some fungi restrict
their attacks to sawn timber.

▲ In fence posts,
sapwood rots away to
leave the heartwood core.

▼ Large mushroom-like
fruiting bodies indicate
fungal infection.

There are many different forms of attack. Some fungi thrive solely on the heartwood of standing timber, leaving behind the characteristic hollow shell. Other species only colonise logs after they're felled, or sawn timber while it's being seasoned. Perhaps the most important group from an economic viewpoint are fungi that attack timber after it's in use. These can be highly damaging, such as dry rot.

Wood rotting and sap stain fungi both belong to a large group of plants that includes mushrooms and toadstools. These large visible signs are actually the fruiting bodies of the fungus, which produce single celled spores and disperse to continue the colonisation. The damage is caused by the vegetative feeding system which is usually invisible on the surface. This system consists of hundreds of fine tube-like structures called hyphae which grow rapidly through the wood structure. They devour both cell walls and contents, eventually developing into a mat-like structure, the mycelium.

Like all living structures, fungi need certain basic conditions in order to survive. Knowing what these are and regulating them gives us a real means of control. There are four requirements:

1 Temperature

The optimum temperature for fungal development is 68-86°F (20–30°C). There is little activity beyond these extremes, which explains the sudden burst of summer activity in temperate regions. Unfortunately, this is also the temperature range which suits us best.

2 Oxygen

For rot to occur there must be an air supply. Fully waterlogged timber rarely decays due to the lack of oxygen. This is why in some countries logs are often stored in water until they're ready for conversion.

3 Moisture

The ideal moisture state for fungal attack is at the fibre saturation point or just above. It's not until wood is dried below about 20 per cent moisture content that you can be sure it's safe from attack. Interestingly, drying infected timber does not necessarily kill the infection. It may just lapse into a dormant state, ready to return if the moisture content rises again. Dry rot is the exception as it usually dies in prolonged dry conditions.

4 Food

The wood itself provides the necessary food source. Fungi actively break down the cell walls as well as their contents, particularly stored carbohydrates in the sapwood. The heartwood of some trees contains extractives which are poisonous to fungi, rendering these species resistant to decay. This would explain why some timbers, such as oak, are naturally durable and why jarrah railway sleepers show no sign of fungal infection or decay even after being exposed to the weather for several years.

▲ **Years of exposure to weathering have little effect on durable timbers.**

▶ **Early stages of pocket rot.**

Each of these conditions must be present for rotting to occur. The lack of just one usually halts the process. Bog oak, for example, is often buried for thousands of years without oxygen. It can be dug up perfectly intact, but starts to fall apart very quickly after being exposed to the drying air.

Types of fungi

The two main constituents of wood are lignin and cellulose, being able to recognize which of these is attacked helps to identify the particular fungus involved. Brown rots feed mainly on cellulose, while white rots feed on both cellulose and lignin. The degree to which either of these substances is affected results in different forms of decay; cubical, spongy or pocket.

The picture above shows a good example of pocket rot. As lignin is the main constituent holding all the wood cells together, anything that attacks it is particularly destructive. A lot of the pigmentation of wood is formed in the lignin, therefore white rots also have a pronounced effect on the colour of the timber. If white rot becomes really advanced, the timber then becomes very pale, soft and spongy.

▼ **Advanced fungal attack leaves the timber soft and spongy.**

▶ **Beefsteak fungus produces beneficial colouring.**

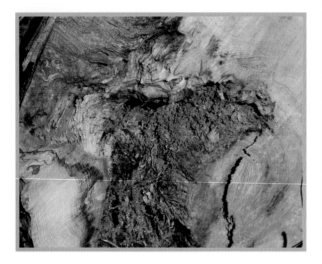

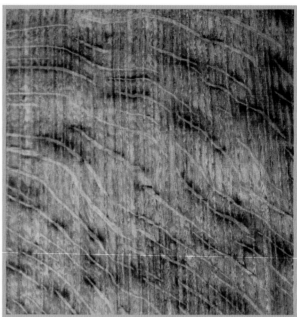

Standing tree fungi

Fungi which attacks standing trees causes high losses for the forest owner. However, this rarely affects timber users, for once seasoned such wood is safe from further decay from this fungi group. The exception is brown oak, normal oak infected by the beefsteak fungus, *Fistulina hepatica*. This gains entry to the tree through a wound, but causes no damage to the living tree apart from extracting nourishment. It does, however, produce chemical changes resulting in the highly prized brown colouration which highlights the wonderful oak figure. This is a rare example of a fungus being beneficial to the woodworker.

Log and timber fungi

Occasionally, trees are felled and left lying around for some time before being converted into planks. Delaying conversion and drying is the prime cause of infection in logs by decaying fungi. This is far worse in tropical countries where warmer temperatures often lead to rapid fungal development. These climates also tend to harbour more in the way of bark-boring insects and ambrosia beetles.

Converted timber which is kept in adverse drying conditions is just as likely to be infected with fungi, particularly those species which don't have naturally resistant heartwood. Again this can sometimes be used

◀ **Logs left lying after felling may start to decay.**

▷ Dry rot spreads rapidly.

▽ Certain timbers
will always rot even
when protected.

to our advantage. The classic fungal staining of
spalted beech, for instance, provides wonderful
examples of decorative figure.

Fungi that attack timber in use

The only sure way to prevent wood rotting fungi
attacking finished products is to only use sound,
kiln-dried material, free from fungal infection and
with sufficient ventilation to prevent it from becoming
damp. The very destructive dry rot thrives in conditions
of relatively low moisture content and any infection
must be treated very seriously. Any wood that is left
in contact with the ground or exposed to the weather
is potentially at risk. The solution is to use more
resistant and usually more expensive timbers, or to
regularly dose everything with preservatives. Yet no
matter what protection is used, susceptible timbers
exposed to extreme conditions will eventually decay.

Spalted wood

The first stage in the decay process is the invasion
of the timber by a variety of fungi. These start to
break down the wood, often producing a variety of
colour changes in the process. When these colour
changes produce decorative effects, yet without
substantial loss of structure, the wood is said to be
spalted. In effect, this is wood in the first stages of
rot. This is nothing new, yet it's only in recent years
that the merits of partly rotted wood as a decorative
material have come to the fore. There is nothing more
spectacular than a highly spalted piece of wood. The
rich intermingling of colours in a kaleidoscope pattern
is almost breathtaking in really extreme examples.

▽ Spalting can produce highly decorative figuring.

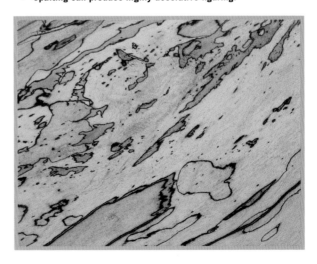

Spalted material is now highly prized.

Pioneer fungi discolours the timber, but has little effect on its strength.

The process

So how does this occur and can we make our own spalted wood? Spalting is a very complicated biological process dependant on a number of interrelated factors. Humidity, temperature, oxygen levels and the exact species of fungi determine the final unique result.

Fungal spores are always floating around us. If one lands on a piece of wood in a suitable state for growth, infection begins. Once the fungus is established, it starts to spread out via a mat-like mass of tiny roots called the mycelium. As the individual strands of the mycelium, the hyphae, grow out they digest the wood. Usually this initial infection by pioneer fungi merely discolours the timber, and has little effect on its strength, although this depends on the species of fungi.

There are dozens of different species involved here, some specific to a particular wood species or group. It's only when another species of fungi joins in that spalting, as opposed to rotting, begins. Each fungus, and there may be many in a single infection, makes its own way through the wood, leaving a different colour

Black zone lines surround the different fungal species.

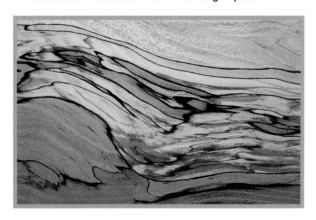

Zone lines vary in width.

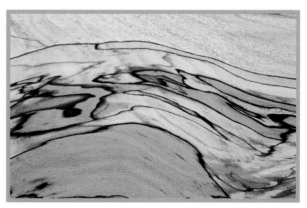

◀ **A distinct boundary between the infected and uninfected timber is possible.**

▼ **It's often difficult to tell if the timber is too badly affected to be usable.**

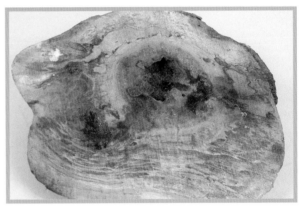

behind it as it goes. When one species comes up against another a black zone line is formed. The pockets of different colours, each surrounded by a black line, is what characterizes spalted wood.

Some infections involve only a couple of species, so the spalting is relatively bland. When several are involved and all intermingle, the zonal lines become much more numerous and decorative. They also vary in width from almost hair-like to several millimetres wide. Spalting is not inevitable, it all depends on the infecting species. One fungus may also subsequently overcome another, usually by producing what are effectively antibiotics, rather than the effect of spalting.

Where spalting does occur, its arrangement does not always follow a specific pattern. Sometimes it follows the direction of the rays, other times there may be a distinct boundary between wood that is spalted and wood that is not. The trick is to use wood that is infected by pioneer fungi and whose composition is still reasonably sound.

The next stage is infection by secondary fungi. These are usually much more specific and totally destroy the timber; nature's way of dealing with fallen material and returning nutrients to the soil. The yellow patches of secondarily decayed timber can be quite decorative, although there is a fine line between the timber being attractive and being unusable.

Both logs and sawn boards can also be infected by fungi, as shown by fruiting bodies such as toadstools or brackets. However, the spread of fungi through the log is much slower and logs, which are often quite spalted at one end, may actually be clean at the other.

▼ **Fruiting bodies indicate the wood rotting fungi within.**

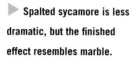
▶ Spalted sycamore is less dramatic, but the finished effect resembles marble.

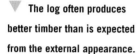
▼ The log often produces better timber than is expected from the external appearance.

▼ Too much secondary infection makes the timber 'punky' and unusable.

Susceptibility

Light coloured woods are usually more susceptible to infection and consequently spalting, as they have less natural resistance, a property usually imparted by the coloured extractives in the heartwood of dark timbers. Therefore beech, sycamore and maple will spalt readily. Sycamore, for example, rarely develops much in the way of zonal lines, usually just discolouring instead. Yet when polished, sycamore can almost look like marble. The darker species, like walnut or elm, are less likely to spalt. This usually only occurs when they're infected by a specific fungus, which can overcome the toxic effect of their extractives.

By keeping your eyes open, you will often notice standing trees which are obviously spalted. These logs usually turn out better than you might think. Although too much secondary infection makes the timber really soft and 'punky', therefore virtually unusable. The degree of rot varies throughout, so it's very unusual to find a log with consistent and uniform spalting.

DIY

So can you spalt your own wood? I've tried several times over the years with mixed results. Wrapping wet material in a plastic bag to encourage the humid conditions necessary for fungal infection rarely seems to work well in practice. People have reported some success, but spalting takes years to develop properly. Although you can induce it to some extent, you cannot get the full effect by speeding up the process.

Regardless of the extent of the initial infection, the whole process of decay grinds to a halt as soon as the wood is dried. There is no danger of items turned from spalted wood continuing to rot. Once it's dry, and kept dry, any spalting will be held in check.

Difficulties

Using spalted wood can cause problems. In a well-figured piece the different colours, each produced by a different fungal species, leave the wood with different densities. Consequently, when you come to work with it some cuts cleanly, other parts rip slightly, while still others pull out in chunks. However sound the material, you will need a lot of abrasive to attain a really clean surface. If there is a particularly soft patch, you can attempt to stabilize it. Previously I used lots of cellulose sealer to do this, now I use very thin cyanoacrylate glue. This is flooded over the soft patch, so that it penetrates into the surface, which can then be worked. The same process needs to be repeated several times as you get near to the finished surface.

Spalted wood can also be tricky to season. If it's evenly infected and discoloured, then all the stresses have been equalized. Yet if the spalting is more varied, or particularly bad in definite planes, splits may develop along the boundaries as the drying stresses overcome the weakened timber.

Dust from spalted wood is often cited as a particular health hazard. I have not seen any scientific evidence to show that this dust is any more injurious than dust from 'normal' wood. Yet I do know that they are both potentially hazardous, so I always wear an air fed helmet for protection, as well as using an air cleaner, when turning spalted wood. Possibly it's the greater amount of sanding it requires which gives us the impression that it's more harmful. These fungal spores are always present in the air, so I consider this extra health risk to be a bit of a red herring.

▶ Some insect species only attack the sapwood.

Solutions

There are no specific techniques involved when working with spalted timber, other than sharp tools and plenty of patience. The continual tearing of the soft parts causes real frustration, particularly when a fine finishing cut leaves a super smooth surface, but also a couple of deep tears. Attempting to fill these tears often simply highlights the problem; there's no alternative to plenty of sanding. The only snag is that the different densities sand out unevenly, the soft areas often become quite hollow compared to the surrounding timber. Use a powered sanding pad to even this out and to spread the load more evenly.

Although many woods will spalt, the prime candidate in this country is beech, providing nicely figured, yet expensive pieces. Many sawmillers, especially those from the 'pre-turning revolution', are bemused by this sudden insatiable demand for material that was previously burnt or just left to rot; it's amazing how fashions change.

Insect damage

The term 'worm' is often used to describe damage caused by a variety of insects which burrow into the wood. As well as spoiling its appearance, these tunnels and holes often reduce the strength of the wood. Some insects will only attack a living tree or green logs, while

▶ **Infection may not become apparent for some time after the timber is in use.**

others focus entirely on seasoned wood or sapwood. It's important to be able to recognize the various types of infestation, as those that occur in wet timber are of less concern if the wood is to be dried in due course. The species that attack dried timber are more of a concern as these can occur at any time.

Beetles

Most wood boring insects are beetles, although much of the damage is done during their larval stage. Beetles have a distinct life cycle that may last for several years. They start off as an egg laid in the timber. This turns into a larva, what we erroneously call a 'worm', which burrows through the wood to feed itself as it grows. It eventually emerges from the timber as an adult beetle, leaving behind the characteristic single exit hole with a mass of damaging tunnels below the surface.

Some of the beetles work in association with fungi. While laying its eggs in the timber, the beetle can often introduce a fungus which is then used to feed its larvae. This fungus decays the wood allowing the beetle, rather than its larvae, to tunnel into it.

If the life cycle of a particular insect is a long one, the infestation may have been happening for some time before it's discovered. It often only emerges after the timber has been used, by which time treatment is too late and the only option is to stop it spreading further. For those insects with a shorter life cycle, the signs are usually more immediately obvious, so treatment can be carried out quickly to halt the infestation.

Common furniture beetles

The most frequent insect attack on wood comes from common furniture beetles, *Anobium punctatum*. These attack seasoned softwood and the sapwood of hardwood timber, only spreading to the heartwood if there is a fungal infection. This beetle has a three to five year life cycle, so it's some time before the exit holes start to appear in the finished timber.

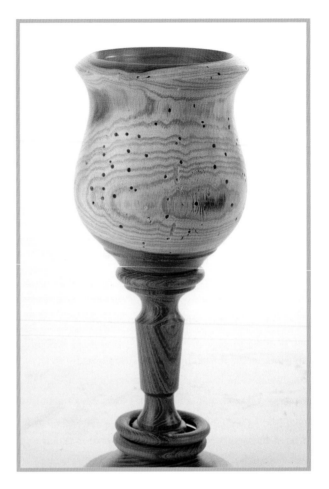

◀ **Common furniture beetle.**

The female will lay up to 80 eggs in cracks or old flight holes in timber or dead trees. The adult is $1/8 - 5/32$ in (3–4mm) in length with a hunched thorax which partially obscures the head. The larvae tunnel along the grain producing a distinctive granular 'frass' or dust that fills the tunnels. They prefer cooler and slightly damp conditions, which is why the incidence is less in modern, centrally heated homes. Adult beetles emerge in early summer when the weather becomes warmer, leaving an exit hole $3/64 - 5/64$ in (1–2mm) in diameter.

Control is difficult as it relies on the application of a suitable solvent-based preservative that rarely penetrates deep enough to kill the active larvae. Although it does kill them when they eat through the surface layers and emerge.

◀ **Death watch beetle.**

◀ **Powder post beetle.**

Death watch beetles

Related to but less common than the common furniture beetle is the death watch beetle, *Xestobium rufovillosum*. It's slightly larger at $^3/_{16}$–$^9/_{32}$ in (5–7mm) in length, with the adults being a dark reddish brown with yellow scale-like hairs on the upper body and wing cases. After mating, the female lays three or four eggs in cracks in the wood surface. These will hatch within a few weeks into $^3/_8$ in (10mm), creamy white and hook shaped larvae with dark brown jaws and golden hair.

Death watch beetles tend to confine attacks to hardwoods, preferring old and partly decaying timber with a high moisture content. They usually start in the sapwood, spreading quickly to the heartwood. The tunnels are about $^1/_8$ in (3mm) in diameter and contain much coarser frass. Their life cycle varies depending on the prevalent conditions. Usually it's one year, but it may stretch to five if conditions are more favourable.

Realistically, control is restricted to removing old infected timber, replacing it with pressure treated alternatives and then eliminating the damp conditions which favour fungal decay and allow re-infestation.

House longhorn beetles

Fortunately rarer but still a serious pest is the house longhorn beetle, *Hylotrupes bajulus,* which usually attack the sapwood of softwood species, even when fully dry. The adults vary in length from $^5/_{16}$–1in (8–25mm). They are black or brown and covered with greyish hairs on their upper body and wing cases. A unique identifying feature is the two shiny black spots on the thorax which resemble eyes. The larvae are greyish white and can grow up to 1$^3/_8$in (35mm) in length. Unfortunately these beetles have a life cycle of up to 10 years, so they can cause serious damage before the infestation becomes obvious. The large flight holes are characteristically oval, about $^3/_{16}$ x $^{11}/_{32}$ in (5 x 9mm) in size with frass in the form of fine round pellets.

Powder post beetles

Insect attacks on wet logs and freshly sawn timber in stick are not a significant problem in the UK, with the exception of the severe attacks by the lyctus beetle, better known as the powder post beetle. These beetles are $^5/_{32}$–$^9/_{32}$ in (4–7mm) long, reddish brown, with a narrow flattened body. The females lay 30–50 eggs in the wide pores of hardwood which hatch in about two weeks. The larvae are creamy white and approximately $^1/_4$ in (6mm) in length. The two most common species in the UK are *Lyctus linearis* and *Lyctus brunneus.*

Their larvae tend to live on the starch content of the sapwood rather than the wall substance itself. They also restrict themselves to certain timbers, with ash, elm, oak and walnut being prime examples. They can do serious damage to stacks of hardwoods held in stick in the open air or even in drying sheds. Fine textured timbers, like beech and sycamore, are more immune, as are coarse textured timbers which lack the necessary starch content.

These beetles do not attack wet timber, but wait until the wood starts to dry before beginning their invasion, consequently they are particularly active during the warmer months. Their typical life cycle is around one year with the beetles emerging in May, although it may be shorter in warmer indoor storage sheds. If starch supplies are limited, the life cycle may extend to several years. Interestingly, the starch content of timber can be reduced and the timber immunized by prolonged storage in water, although this is often not a commercial option.

◀ **House longhorn beetle.**

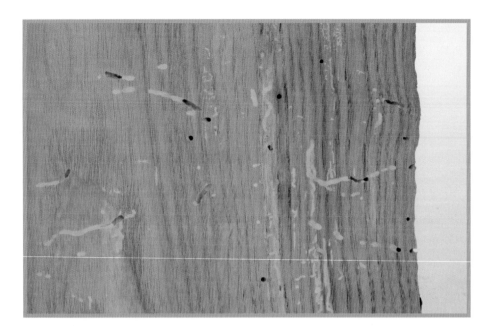

◀ **Powder post beetle attack.**

The tunnels of the powder post beetles all run parallel to the grain, with separate galleries merging together as the attack progresses. Eventually, the entire interior of the infected wood is reduced to a flour-like powder. Flight holes are about ¹⁄₁₆ in (1.5mm) in diameter and are often confused with those of the common furniture beetle, although close examination of the frass shows it to be much finer. Removal of susceptible sapwood is the most efficient control measure, but chemical control is possible via annual spraying of timber stacks with an insecticide just before the beetles are due to emerge. There is another family of powder post beetles, the Bostryychidae. These are slightly larger and tend to be pests of tropical rather than temperate regions.

Pin hole borers

These beetles belong to two families, the Scolytidae and the Platypodidae. These are slightly different in that the larvae live on ambrosia, a unique fungus introduced into the tunnels bored by the adult beetles, rather than by larvae; hence they're often given the name ambrosia beetles. These beetles tunnel into trees or green logs at right angles to the grain, with the tunnels showing a characteristic black colouration on the walls. The surrounding tissue may also be discoloured. As the fungus which feeds the larvae requires moisture, it cannot survive in timber that's starting to dry, so this pest is normally confined to logs. Although it can cause considerable damage, it's immediately obvious once the log is converted and there is no risk of further attack. Damage is also normally confined to tropical species.

Other beetles

There are a variety of other beetles, weevils and moths capable of damaging timber, yet many of these are a secondary infection following some form of initial fungal attack that weakened the timber. Although an attack from these lesser species is inconvenient,

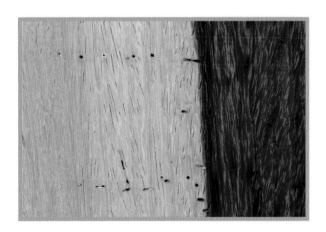

◀ **Effects of pin hole borers.**

◀ **Bark beetle.**

it's rarely a significant problem. Unbarked softwood left outside may be attacked by the bark borer, *Ernobius mollis,* which causes damage to rustic work, such as sheds and pergolas.

Treatment

Most timbers can be treated with a range of insecticides and fungicides, but the results are often variable as it's difficult to get these substances to penetrate into the surface. Control of external conditions is more effective in the case of fungi, as few can survive without moisture. Insects are most susceptible when they're in the adult stage and flying around, so identifying and spraying repeatedly around emergence times offers the best hope of preventing re-infestation. There is often little you can do for current infestations and the damage is usually done by the time it's discovered.

Unfortunately, many of the chemicals are expensive and not particularly user friendly. A better line of attack therefore is good housekeeping with stored timber and sterilization within a kiln. A few hours exposure at 149°F (65°C) can eradicate most problems, although it can't guarantee that an attack won't occur again.

Termites

Fortunately termites are unable to survive in the UK, instead they're restricted to tropical regions. This is fortunate as they are probably the most damaging timber pest in the world. Termites have a voracious appetite for dry wood, hollowing out timber structures to leave an outer shell of wood. No wood is immune to termites, yet some species are more resistant. Often this resistance is contrary to that of fungal attack. Species resistant to fungi, for example, are often less resistant to termites and vice versa. The hardness of the timber has no bearing on termite resistance.

Marine borers

These are not insects, but rather work-like creatures capable of doing severe damage to timber submerged in salt water. The best-known is the toredo, *Toredo navalis,* which is most active in tropical regions. No timber is resistant to this creature, even species like greenheart or those with a high silica content. The worm, which can be up to 4in (102mm) long and ½in (13mm) in diameter, peppers the wood with burrows that can be up to 1in (25mm) in diameter.

Another marine creature is the gribble *Limmnoria lignorum* which looks similiar to a large woodlouse. This eats away at the surface of submerged timber creating shallow burrows that are constantly broken open by the action of the waves causing extremely rapid deterioration.

Isolation from the water, usually by encasing the submerged timber in a metal sleeve, is about the only failsafe method of prevention.

▶ **Damage to submerged timber by marine borers.**

Timber Properties

The physical structure of the different cells and tissues, their chemical composition as well as the way in which they're arranged, significantly influences the overall usefulness of the resulting timber. It's worth looking at a few of the main characteristics to observe how this interaction works in practice.

Sapwood and heartwood

We have already highlighted the definite distinction between sapwood and heartwood in most timbers; with sapwood usually being lighter in colour and less durable. Logs usually contain 25–35 per cent sapwood, even more in some tropical species. Therefore if the sapwood is not going to be used, there is often a lot of potential waste.

There is very little difference between the weight of dry sapwood and dry heartwood at the same moisture content. The exceptions are those timbers with a high extractives content and therefore slightly heavier heartwood. However, sapwood has a higher moisture content, so is heavier than heartwood. The strength properties are also very similar, with sapwood being just marginally weaker than heartwood at the same moisture level.

Durability reveals marked differences, although the requirements vary depending on the geographical location. In the UK's predominantly wet climate, durability is more determined by resistance to fungal attack and weathering. In tropical countries, resistance to insect infestation is a more likely measure of durability. As sapwood is rich in sugars, it's attractive to both insects and fungi, although both pests target specific species. Heartwood, on the other hand, often contains extractives that are toxic to both fungi and

insects, so is likely to be more durable. However, heartwood is not totally immune and is sometimes targeted by specific wood rotting fungi which hollow out the tree leaving only a narrow ring of living sapwood, a feature that may not be visible from the outside.

The structural changes occurring in the various cells during their transformation from sapwood to heartwood result in the heartwood becoming far less permeable and more resistant to stains and preservatives. This is probably insignificant, unless you are looking for an even stain on a board containing both heartwood and sapwood. We've already seen that heartwood is less susceptible to insect attack, so its relative impermeability to preservatives is therefore not important.

▶ Tropical species often have large sapwood bands.

Sapwood can be used alongside heartwood, as long as you bear these properties in mind. Colour is the prime consideration, but if this is not an issue, durability is probably the determining factor. Avoid using sapwood for outdoor use unless it has been treated with preservative, in which case it should be just as durable as heartwood. For internal use or in dry conditions, sapwood can be used safely. In certain species, for example ash, the white sapwood is preferable for uses such as the production of sports goods, although the darker heartwood is just as strong.

Growth rings

The distribution of growth rings within the timber is an important factor, determining strength and many of the working characteristics. The width of the rings is an illustration of the speed of growth. The rate of growth is measured in terms of the number of rings per inch or 2.5cm. The rings are also an immediate visual indication of the likely strength of the wood.

The growth rate is measured by the number of annual rings per inch or 2.5cm.

▶ **The proportion of latewood to earlywood determines the strength of the timber.**

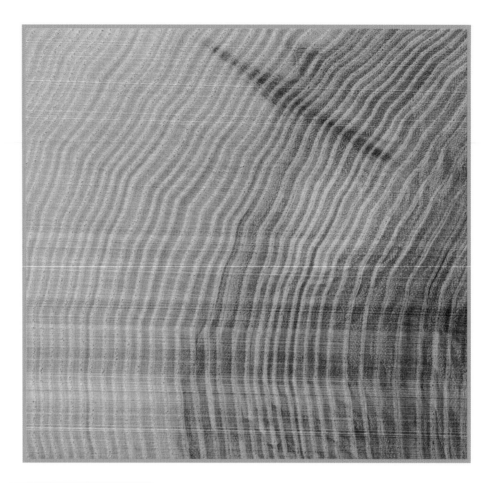

▼ **Ring widths also affect the working properties.**

With the ring porous hardwoods, the distinct variations within the annual rings are determined by the different proportions of early and latewood. The diffuse porous species lack this distinction as the ring composition remains the same no matter how wide it is.

In all timbers, very narrow or very wide rings result in weaker material. There is an optimum growth rate to maximize strength which varies from species to species. Generally, the optimum in softwoods is 10–20 rings per inch and for ring porous hardwoods it's 5–10 rings. The proportion of latewood is key here as it's much stronger than the very open structured earlywood.

Strength is not the only characteristic affected by ring width. For a lot of woodworking applications, the working qualities are much more important. For example, very narrow ringed material, although weaker, is often seen as far superior because of how easily it works and finishes. Careful selection of your material to suit the eventual use is often a trade-off of strength versus working properties.

▼ Knots are formed when a branch grows out from the side of the tree.

▶ Knots become a problem if the branch dies and starts to decay.

◀ Dead knots may decay away totally leaving a void.

Knots

To the majority of woodworkers, knots are regarded as a defect. Yet in some cases, they can be quite decorative. It simply depends on the type and distribution of the knot. These features are formed when a branch grows out from the side of the tree and the surrounding trunk tissue gradually encases its base. Where the branch is still living, its tissue becomes continuous with the stem resulting in live knots that are as strong, if not stronger, than the rest of the wood.

Knots only become a problem if the branch dies or is cut off. Then, the surrounding tissue continues to encase the area, yet the two tissues are no longer continuous resulting in a dead or loose knot often with a bark pocket. This dead knot may even decay away within the tree to leave a void. The pictures show a low-grade softwood peeled into sheets, so that the knot is repeated in a regular pattern. It's fascinating to cut through a log which has had its branches pruned back at some stage. Although invisible from the outside, the evidence of many years of growth is buried beneath.

▶ **The grain in the tissue around the knot is often at right angles making machining difficult.**

There are many reasons why knots are seen as defects. Firstly, the grain of the knot is usually at right angles to the surrounding tissue making all machining difficult and often ending up being pulled out. Secondly, the rate of shrinkage is greater across the knot than in the perpendicular surrounding timber, so the knot may loosen of its own accord or develop radial cracks.

On the other hand, knots are not always a problem. They can sometimes be a decorative feature. Small ones in cocobolo, for example, often produce wonderful three dimensional effects. The extreme example of thousands of tiny knots in the burr of an elm or walnut, as shown in the picture below right, also produces some magnificent patterns.

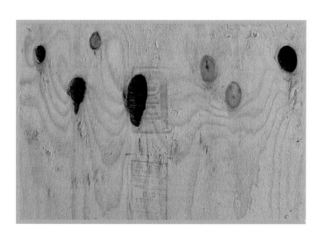

▶ **Tiny knots in elm produce magnificent patterns.**

◀ **Sheathing ply usually creates a regular pattern of knots in the peeled veneer.**

Juvenile wood

There are many other examples of abnormal wood growth that can be easily explained in terms of tree development. One type which is common in softwoods, but rare in hardwoods, is juvenile wood. The first few rings of growth around the pith of the tree are often of totally different quality to the rest. When a young tree grows quickly without competition, the initial wood is characterized by wide rings of low density. This shrinks unevenly during the drying process and also warps more readily. If possible avoid juvenile wood because of its unpredictability. This is another good reason for avoiding any timber that contains the very centre of the tree.

▲ Juvenile wood should be avoided if possible.

▶ Compression wood is found underneath a leaning branch in softwoods.

Reaction wood

Another interesting wood tissue is reaction wood which is always found in leaning stems and branches. This is nature's response to the uneven gravitational pull of the angled growth, attempting to straighten it up again.

Reaction wood is totally different in softwoods than in hardwoods. In softwood conifers it forms on the underneath of the leaning branch and is referred to as compression wood. The picture above shows a branch of softwood yew, with a huge amount of compression wood distorting its shape. In hardwood, reaction wood forms on the top of the branches and

◀ Tension wood on the top of the leaning branch is usually less marked.

▶ **Tension wood is difficult to machine without tearing.**

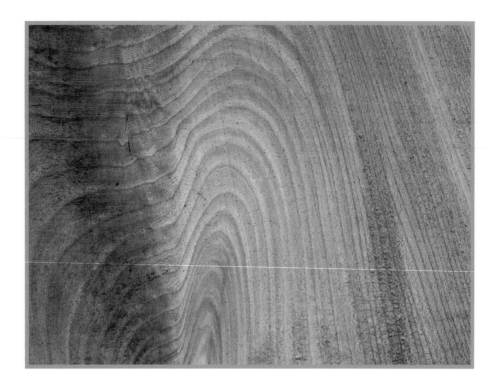

is called tension wood. This is always less marked than compression wood and the pith is usually less off centre.

Reaction wood can easily be explained through a closer look at the cell anatomy. In compression wood, hormones are produced by the uneven gravitational pull. This stimulates the tracheids and causes them to grow abnormally in the latewood part of the ring. There are two important consequences of this for woodworkers. Firstly, the much thicker tracheid walls mean that the wood is much denser, yet actually contains less cellulose so it is in fact weaker. It also tends to be darker in colour than the normal tissue and takes stains very unevenly relative to the surrounding tissue. Secondly, reaction wood shrinks very differently. Normal wood tends to shrink longitudinally, whereas compression wood will move up to 25 times more as part of its natural straightening mechanism.

Tension wood is again characterized by uneven growth rings. It's paler than the surrounding tissue, yet is more lustrous when viewed under oblique light. As there is a greater ratio of cellulose to lignin in the cell walls, it tends to be stronger than normal. Yet as the permeability also varies, it's difficult to finish without leaving blotches. In addition, the fibres won't

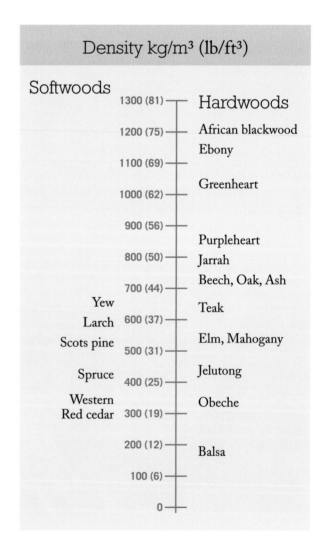

Density kg/m³ (lb/ft³)

Softwoods		Hardwoods
	1300 (81)	
	1200 (75)	African blackwood
		Ebony
	1100 (69)	
		Greenheart
	1000 (62)	
	900 (56)	
		Purpleheart
	800 (50)	Jarrah
		Beech, Oak, Ash
	700 (44)	
Yew		Teak
Larch	600 (37)	
Scots pine		Elm, Mahogany
	500 (31)	
Spruce	400 (25)	Jelutong
Western Red cedar	300 (19)	Obeche
	200 (12)	Balsa
	100 (6)	
	0	

◄◄ **Lignum vitae blank weighs 23oz (650g).**

◄ **The same sized blank in ash weighs just 12oz (350g).**

cut cleanly. Instead they tend to pull out resulting in a faint wooliness, no matter how sharp your tools are or how much you sand.

Density

This is another very important property of wood, largely determining its strength. Dry timber consists of a mixture of solid material making up the cell walls and lots of air in the cell cavities. The ratio of solid mass relative to the volume is usually what is meant by the density. This can be quoted in several different ways. The most common is the ratio of the weight of a set volume of timber to the same volume of water, giving the specific gravity. As this is a simple ratio, there are no units of measurement. For a more direct comparison, density is sometimes quoted as weight per cubic foot or cubic metre, although this assumes that the values are measured at the same moisture content.

Regardless of the tree species, cell wall substance has a specific gravity of about 1.5, around 1½ times heavier than water. Theoretically, a cubic metre of solid wall substance would weigh 3,307lb (1,500kg). Yet different timbers vary between 220lb (100kg) and 2,866lb (1,300kg) per cubic metre. This variation is explained by the different ratios of cell wall to cell cavity in the various woods; the parenchyma cells and thin walled vessels, relative to the amount of thicker walled fibres. This accounts for the large difference in density between equivalent sized pieces of different species of wood.

Many freshly cut timbers have a specific gravity in excess of 1 and will therefore sink in water. It's only as they dry out that the specific gravity drops below 1 and they will begin to float. Even timbers that are mostly air when dry, like balsa, will barely float when wet. The lignum blank in the picture above for example, weighs 23oz (650g) with a specific gravity of around 1.2, even when fully dry. Yet the ash in the righthand picture only weighs 12oz (350g) with a specific gravity of about 0.6. Most timbers are in the range of 0.3 to about 0.7. Although there is variation even within the same species, determined to a large extent by growth rates. Not only does density vary within the same species, it also varies within the same tree. The wood which is highest up the tree has the lowest density and the most marked ring porous species.

Acoustic properties

These are closely linked to the density and the natural elasticity of the wood and are particularly relevant to musical instrument makers. If you strike a piece of wood which is freely suspended it will emit a note, the

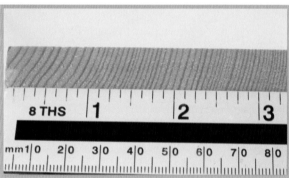

Wooden floorboards are becoming increasingly popular.

Highly figured wood still signifies quality.

Timber for instrument making has an incredibly slow but uniform growth rate.

pitch of which is determined by the natural frequency of vibration. This is controlled by the density which is a feature of the growth pattern. All these qualities are therefore interlinked in a close relationship. For instance, when spruce trees are grown high up in the Swiss Alps, they have an incredibly slow, but uniform growth rate. This leads to superb resonance properties ideal for making high quality musical instrument soundboards. If a wood surface is firmly fixed, it loses elasticity and sound waves are deadened, which is why rooms are often panelled to act as a sound insulator.

Thermal conductivity

This is a minor feature of wood, yet an important one. As so much of the structure is airspace, the worst conductor of heat, wood has a very low thermal conductivity and is always warm to the touch. A nicely shaped piece of wood demands to be touched, which is why tool handles or wooden seating are always more comfortable than their metal equivalents. This apparent warmth produces a feeling of well-being. It also goes a long way to explain why wooden floorboards are making such a comeback and why low-cost furniture is often given the appearance of wood. It's all part of the psychological property of timber, linking the world's most natural material to sensual properties.

There are also definite physical benefits to the low thermal conductivity of wood. For example, wooden doors are much better at preventing a fire spreading than metal equivalents. Even in a severe fire they won't break down because of direct combustion, only if the inevitable shrinkage causes gaps or cracks to appear to allow the flames to spread.

Electrical conductivity

It's virtually impossible to pass an electric current through totally dry wood. As the moisture content increases, so does the ability to pass a current through. This is the principle utilized in electric moisture meters measuring the resistance of currents passed between two electrodes pushed into the wood.

◀ Moisture meters measure the electrical resistance of the timber between the tips of the probe.

Odour

Most wood has a distinct odour. This is usually most noticeable when cutting while wet, but it does remain to some extent in dried material. Some species are chosen specifically for their smell – for example, sandalwood or cedar which are used in drawers as their odours deter moths. A variety of acacia found in Western Australia is very aptly named raspberry jam wood due to its unique odour when cut. Indian rosewood is another sweetly fragrant wood whose smell lingers in the workshop long after you have finished cutting it. As with perfumes, the smell of freshly cut wood is a matter of taste. Although being so unique, smell is often a very useful aid to identification.

Burning properties

Although it has a low thermal conductivity making it relatively inflammable, wood is highly combustible in the right conditions. Yet for it to burn, wood has to reach temperatures of well in excess of 500°F (260°C). With a plentiful supply of oxygen, the gases caused by the breakdown of the wood start to burn and can even generate temperatures up to 2000°F (1093.33°C). However, it's not a particularly efficient fuel.

Different species burn very differently. The heat output depends on a number of factors, the density of the wood, its chemical make up and most importantly, its moisture content. Denser woods will always generate more heat, but lighter woods will also burn well if they have a high resin content. Wet wood is a very poor heat producer as much of the output is lost through evaporation of internal moisture. In order to maximize heat output, firewood needs to be seasoned thoroughly. Although realistically, reducing it to a moisture content of around 20 per cent is usually sufficient. Ash is possibly the only timber that burns well when green, although it still burns better when thoroughly dry.

▼ Firewood needs to be dried to a moisture content below 20 per cent for efficient burning.

Water

Water has the greatest influence on the behaviour of timber. Wood from freshly felled logs contains a large percentage of moisture, and this profoundly influences properties such as weight, strength and stability, as well as the susceptibilty to fungal and insect attack.

Interaction

We've all witnessed the close interaction of water and wood. For example, doors that shut perfectly in the summer, yet bind in the winter; the turned bowl that goes oval, or the perfectly sawn plank which cracks and warps as it dries. These are all dimensional reactions of the wood to changes in the water content, or more specifically changes in relative humidity.

The majority of problems associated with timber involve water in some way or another, so it's important to understand its influence and the application of this knowledge at the workshop level. Once again the cause and effects can be traced back to the timber anatomy, firstly at the cell level and then by looking at the timber as a solid mass.

Wood in trees is literally saturated, with all the cell walls and their internal cavities swollen with water. In situations where we are likely to use wood, either in the round or converted into boards, much of this water will dry out causing some degree of shrinkage. Eventually, a balance is achieved between the drying wood and the surrounding humidity. Yet this balance is dynamic, continually responding to atmospheric changes. There is a constant exchange of moisture between the wood and the surrounding atmosphere. The aim is to dry the wood to a level suitable for its

◀ **Freshly sawn flat boards soon crack and warp as they dry.**

eventual environment in order to pre-shrink it and to maintain this balance, so as to reduce any further dimensional movement.

Moisture content

It's important to know the exact amount of water in a given sample of wood, the moisture content (MC). This varies considerably, but as the entirely dry weight of wood substance is constant we can express the variable property, the MC, as a percentage of the constant property, the dry weight. This ratio is:

$$\frac{\text{Weight of water present in sample}}{\text{Dry weight of wood sample}} \times 100$$

There are many highly complicated ways to precisely determine this ratio, usually using an oven to dry the sample thoroughly or by using a distillation method. A slightly less accurate, yet much more immediate method we could try is a moisture meter. Although they lack precision, these meters are perfectly adequate for measuring the MC accurately enough for us woodworkers to use.

From this simple equation, it's clear that in very wet timbers, with a greater percentage of water by weight than solid material, the MC can actually be in excess of 100 per cent. The MC also varies between the heartwood and sapwood, as well as the different heights of the tree.

It's worth mentioning that there's no evidence to support the theory that sap is highest in a tree during the summer and lowest during the winter. Consequently, a fresh trunk is no drier in winter than it is in the summer. In fact, there is evidence that the reverse is actually true. The only scientific justification for felling in winter is the reduced likelihood of fungal or insect attack, particularly with species like sycamore. The log is also less likely to be degraded by hot drying conditions, encountered in the summer months.

To go any further we need to understand humidity, the general term used to describe the amount of water vapour in the air. We are actually more interested in relative humidity (RH), the ratio of water in the air at a certain temperature relative to the amount it can actually hold. This relationship has a major bearing on everything to do with wood and therefore its behaviour.

◀ **Water can be squeezed out of timber like a sponge.**

Fibre saturation point

We've previously seen that wood cells are hollow and in a living tree often completely filled with water. With the cavities in the timber full with water, the tissue itself is also fully saturated. Let's use the analogy of comparing freshly felled timber to a soaking wet sponge. If we squeeze the sponge, water runs out of the cavities. You can also do this with a piece of wood, to allow free water to be released. Yet even when it's fully wrung out, the tissue remains damp.

Although all the water has left the cell cavities, some still remains within the cell walls, this is called the 'fibre saturation point' (FSP). This water is chemically attached and is referred to as bound water. Most timbers can hold up to 30 per cent of their dry weight in this state. It's this bound water that is the most difficult to remove in the later stages of seasoning.

Wood above the FSP is weak but stable. It's only as it begins to dry below this point that shrinkage and movement start to occur, yet it also gains in strength. Obviously the drier the surrounding atmosphere, or more accurately the lower the RH, the more bound water is lost over all.

The picture on the right shows a piece of ash 10in (257mm) in diameter and 5in (125mm) thick, which I recently unearthed in a rather damp shed.

I actually rough cut this in 1978, when its fresh weight was 13lb 6oz (6.17kg). Some 30 years later, much of the water has been lost, so it now weighs 10lb 4oz (4.72kg). The amount of water lost is shown in the bottle; it makes you wonder just where it all comes from. Interestingly, my moisture meter still showed it to be 21 per cent, a result which is totally expected and easily explained.

▼ **The amount of water the rough cut blank has lost over 30 years is shown in the bottle.**

▶ **Wood in three stages of use, all of which have shrunk and distorted.**

EMC

Wood is hygroscopic, losing bound water to a low RH, but gaining it again at higher RHs. At any given RH and temperature there is a specific moisture content of the wood when no interchange takes place, this is the 'equilibrium moisture content' (EMC). If the temperature is kept constant, the EMC will increase as the RH increases. It will also conversely decrease as the RH decreases. To illustrate this, I re-weighed the blank shown in the picture on the left a few days after bringing it into a drier atmosphere; it had lost another 6oz (170g). This point is fundamental to understanding the process of drying wood.

There is an interesting inconsistency here, as the EMC at a given temperature is not constant. Instead it varies according to whether the wood is drying out or gaining moisture to reach the equilibrium. This is called the 'hysteresis effect', where the EMC gained by losing bound water is higher than that achieved through reabsorbing water at the same temperature. This is a fascinating anomaly and a reminder that wood is a highly developed material.

This equilibrium effect puts pay to the common misconception that once wood has been dried, in particular kiln-dried, it's then perfectly stable and irreversibly dry. In fact, even after drying to a very low moisture content, it will reabsorb bound water to the EMC if it's stored in damp conditions. It's no good assuming that just because a piece of wood has been in stock for many years that it's dry, it probably isn't! It all depends on the surrounding humidity at the time.

There is another crucial point to consider with reference to drying and seasoning. It's only when moisture is lost below the FSP, referred to as the bound water, that there are any dimensional changes to the timber. It's important to differentiate between the two distinct types of change. The first occurs as the wood dries out from its totally saturated, freshly felled state to a seasoned condition, this is covered by the term 'shrinkage'. The picture above shows wood in three different stages of use. In all three, the wood has shrunk as a result of drying down to the EMC, resulting in a dimensional change. Smaller changes occur as a result of local variations in RH, this is 'movement', as in the case I described earlier when a door sticks and then eases as the seasons change.

Timber with a moisture content above the FSP is totally stable. This is perhaps a good place to clear up the distinction between green and freshly sawn timber. Green is often used to describe freshly cut timber, when it actually refers to timber with a moisture content higher than the FSP, regardless of when it was cut.

Shrinkage

This is the property that causes us woodworkers most problems. Yet every piece of timber behaves in a relatively predictable way, so by understanding the basic principles we should be able to anticipate much of what is likely to happen. Having said this, the degree of dimensional change may vary, depending on factors such as the orientation of the wood cells or the presence of reaction wood and extractives.

▶ **Longitudinal shrinkage is normally minimal.**

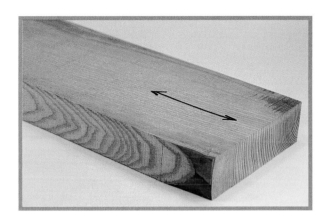

Shrinkage is measured along the three main axes, longitudinal, tangential and radial. It's expressed as a percentage of the green dimensions, as shown by the following formula:

$$\text{Shrinkage} = \frac{\text{Green dimension} - \text{totally dry dimension}}{\text{Green dimension}} \times 100$$

Even when wood dries from above the FSP to a completely dry state, the longitudinal shrinkage is very small, usually only about 0.1 per cent. However, in juvenile wood or reaction wood it may be 2 or even 3 per cent, up to 30 times that of normal wood. It's important to remain aware of this when using any abnormal wood tissues, as these can crack and distort where you least expect it.

Shrinkage in the other two planes however is much more significant. Tangential shrinkage, at right angles to the grain but parallel to the annual rings, is always the most dramatic, averaging around 7 per cent

and reaching as high as 12 per cent in beech. The bowl in the picture below clearly demonstrates this effect. There is a ½in (13mm) difference across the width of the bowl relative to the length.

Radial shrinkage, which is at right angles to the rings, is less severe. It commonly reaches 2–4 per cent, although it can reach up to 5–6 per cent. For most timbers, whether softwood or hardwood, the ratio of tangential to radial shrinkage is nearly always in the region of 1.7, although with some species it varies considerably. Holly at about 2.1 is notoriously unstable, while yew at 1.3 is much more forgiving.

This difference between radial and tangential shrinkage is entirely due to the inherent anatomical structure, particularly the restricting effect of the rays

▼ **Juvenile or reaction wood may crack and distort where you least expect it.**

▼ **Shape changes due to shrinkage.**

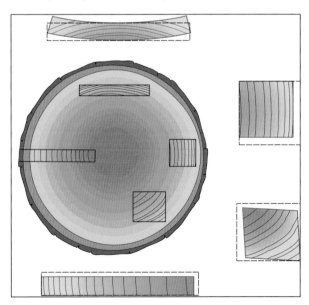

▼ Tangential shrinkage is always more dramatic.

▶ Radial shrinkage is normally less severe.

and the differing amounts of lignification in the various cell walls. It's the amount of this differential shrinkage that determines many of the seasoning defects which will be covered in more in detail in the next chapter.

Movement

These dimensional changes are always much less than those of shrinkage. They're also directly related to immediate changes in the surrounding environment, particularly RH. The clock below right, for example, was fine for years until it was re-hung over a radiator. The change in RH brought about a change in the EMC, resulting in a dimensional change significant enough to buckle its face. We've all experienced this phenomenon in one way or another. A panelled door, for example, may suddenly open if the environment changes either permanently or on a seasonal basis.

Like shrinkage, the values for movement vary from species to species. They broadly follow the same trends, with some interesting variations. Oak, for example, shrinks quite significantly, but moves very little. Whereas ramin shrinks very little, but will move considerably. The origin of this variation is uncertain, but it's thought to be linked to the difference in EMC between species at a given relative humidity. High temperatures during seasoning can reduce the final EMC and consequently reduce subsequent movement.

Obviously, we would prefer timber with low movement values as panels remain more stable and turned bowls stay circular. Yet often dimensionally stable timbers are not particularly attractive as regards to figure. The drying process is all about accepting inevitable changes and attempting to minimize the factors likely to cause problems later on.

◀ Tangential shrinkage is exemplified in this rough turned bowl.

▶ Dimensional changes can still occur after the timber has been worked.

Drying Wood

The science behind why timber needs to be dried before use should now be clear, but how does this apply in practice? When you're presented with a pile of wet boards, how do you maximize the final amount of usable timber that will behave in the way you would expect?

Background knowledge

Firstly, we need to clarify the terms 'seasoning' and 'drying', which are often used synonymously. Seasoning is the process of conditioning wood to a state suitable for its eventual environment, while drying is one of these conditioning factors. Seasoned timber is superior for virtually all purposes, yet the description conveys the impression that some mystical transformation has taken place. It also suggests that the longer the wood is left to season, the better the resulting timber, particularly with regard to stability. From the preceding chapters, it's obvious that this is not true. All we need to do is to remove the excess moisture and the quicker this is done, without degrade, the better.

The main objective of seasoning is to produce stable timber which can be used for its chosen purpose with little or no appreciable movement. Getting it to this stage brings other advantages. Many of the staining and rotting fungi only survive if the moisture content is above 20 per cent. Therefore, seasoning halts any incipient decay and prevents infection in clean timber. This is why it's safe to use spalted timbers. The rotting fungi which produce the fabulous staining effects thrive on wet logs, but are unable to survive as soon as the moisture content falls. However, even when a piece of wood has been seasoned, there's nothing to stop it becoming re-infected if the moisture content rises again.

The effectiveness of any finish as well as many of the glues are highly dependant on the moisture content of the wood. Most of these will only work successfully if the surface is dry, so seasoning is vital.

More relevant to those of us who are using wood structurally is the fact that timber actually gains strength as it dries. Cleaving a trunk of dry wood then cleaving a wet trunk will illustrate just what a difference seasoning can make. On a smaller scale, firewood is much easier to split when it's freshly felled.

▶ **Logs need to be converted into usable sections before use.**

Added complications

When insects are involved the situation becomes much more complicated. Some species only live in green timber and quickly disappear as the moisture content falls during seasoning, while others thrive in dry wood. Therefore, moisture content does not necessarily guarantee immunity.

Determining factors

The process of drying and ultimately seasoning timber relies on the balance between moisture leaving the surface of the timber and the movement of this moisture from the interior to the surface. This balance is dependant on three factors: the humidity of the surrounding air, the movement of that air and, most influentially, the ambient temperature. By controlling these three the wood should season timber perfectly. Unfortunately, it's always much simpler in theory than in reality. Various strategies have been devised to control these factors and their interactions, from this evolved the art of timber seasoning.

The evaporation of water from the surface is determined by the surrounding relative humidity; the lower it is the more easily it takes up moisture. However, as the relative humidity rises, the air is less able to take up moisture and drying begins to slow or even cease. Air movement and temperature are therefore important factors in the control of humidity.

These factors are all harnessed in one of two main methods of seasoning: air or kiln. These are sometimes referred to as natural and artificial respectively, although this suggests that kiln-dried timber is in some way inferior to air-dried. Provided the process has been carried out correctly, kiln-dried timber should have the same working properties as air-dried, you will just get there a lot quicker.

Whichever method you use, it's virtually impossible to season material in the round. It nearly always ends in failure, eventually if not immediately. A nice pile of logs may look suitable for use in large sections straight from the trunk, but they must be cut first. There is something magical about seeing beautiful boards come slicing off a log and accumulating in a stack. It's a pity they don't always stay this way. From this stage on it's down to the drying process and how well it's controlled.

◁ **There is something magical about beautiful boards slicing off a log.**

◀ A wood store for
air drying only needs
to provide basic shelter.

▼ Continued exposure
to water can seriously
discolour the boards.

◀ Few of us can afford the
luxury of a large drying shed.

Air drying

This is all about utilizing the power of the sun and
the wind to dry the timber, while still protecting it
from the rain. Air drying is a science in itself with
many different books having been written on the
subject, setting out piling techniques, stack dimensions,
as well as site orientation. Little of this is possible
or even relevant to us small-scale users, but irrelevant
of the scale the basic principles are the same.

A woodstore can be rigged up out of virtually
anything. However crude, as long as it provides basic
shelter it will work. In my experience, it's the sun that
does the majority of damage during air seasoning.

Dramatic localized temperature changes always cause
surface checking, so provide shade in the form of a top
cover if possible.

Controlling the elements is key. Wind provides
the air movement necessary to prevent the atmosphere
becoming saturated, while the sun provides heat to
lower the relative humidity and to maintain the drying
gradient. Provided your timber is well-protected, rain
has little effect, other than increasing humidity and
therefore slowing down the process. However, rain
falling onto the timber itself can nullify all your efforts.
The timber may also soak up water rapidly causing it
to become seriously discoloured. The occasional shower
is less important.

Ideally, the wood should be piled up in a properly-
ventilated purpose-built drying shed. However, few of
us can afford such a luxury, both in terms of cost and
space. In addition, not even the best shed is perfect,
as it cannot directly control the natural variations in
climate and consequently humidity. The way the timber
is stacked, and therefore the way that the air circulates
around it, is a more effective means of control.

▼ **Successive boards must be separated by stickers.**

▶ **Even a small stack may use several hundred stickers.**

▶ **Stickers need to be positioned carefully to provide maximum support and to prevent sagging.**

Stickers

Successive boards are separated by small strips of wood called stickers; the thicker the stickers the faster the air flow. These are usually around $^{25}/_{32}$ in (20mm) square, although timbers that are prone to face checking may require thinner stickers to slow down the drying rate. Stickers should not be too wide or the area underneath them may become stained as it's prevented from drying out properly. Yet if they're too narrow, the surfaces of the boards can become bruised. It's surprising just how many stickers you need. A large timber yard with hundreds of logs 'in stick' will invest hugely in stickers, so they're treated with care and reused several times.

How close together the stickers are placed is also important. Due to the fact that they restrict airflow, there should be as few as possible, yet too few can cause the boards to sag. Effectively, it depends on the thickness of the planks and their liability to warp. 1in (25mm) thick boards, for example, will need stickers every 24in (600mm) or so. For boards above 2in (50mm) it increases to 20in (1000mm).

Sticker with care

Ideally, all the stickers should be kept in neat vertical rows to prevent distortion of the boards. Although this is not always strictly observed, it's worth the effort, particularly with thinner material.

▷ **Stacking is easy if the log is cut to just one thickness.**

Boards must be stickered as quickly as possible after cutting. 'Close piling', when the boards are re-stacked together without any stickers, always causes staining even if they're only left for a few days. Some species are very prone to fungal staining so, even with immediate stickering, they benefit from having sawdust brushed off them before piling for air-drying. Sycamore is the classic example as this has to be end reared or stacked on end to avoid any disfiguring sticker marks.

All wood, no matter what the species, tends to change colour as it dries. This is caused by a chemical reaction between the moist air and the pigments that are drawn out of the timber. Obviously, this occurs less where the stickers are and the drying is slower. Plus, the subsequent sticker marks are usually only found in the top surface and will clean off easily enough.

◁ **Close piled, successive boards re-stacked without stickers.**

Stacking

How you stack the log for drying really depends on the way it's cut. A large-scale user can afford to have all the log cut to one thickness to make stacking easier. This is further simplified if the boards are also square edged. As small-scale users we often require a variety of thicknesses from a single log, especially as it's probably enough to keep us going for years!

The picture below shows a nice cherry log cut to woodturning sizes, but left waney edged for maximum conversion, although stacking is now more awkward. In theory, the larger boards should be stacked on top

◁ **Sycamore is easily stained by the incorrect use of stickers.**

△ **Small-scale users will probably require several thicknesses from a single log.**

◀ Stacks need to be kept neat and tidy to maximize airflow.

to keep the thinner ones from warping. I've never been convinced by this theory. Personally, I like to see stresses in the wood emerge during drying in the form of distortion. You can then work around the results knowing that the stress is gone, rather than have the wood warp later as you work it.

Keep the stacks neat and tidy to maximize airflow. Loose boards simply discolour, then crack and are eventually wasted. Good housekeeping is essential in your timber store, regardless of the time it takes for the timber to dry. Finally, inspect the stacks regularly to check for insects, these are particularly prone in species such as cherry and laburnum.

As air drying is such an inexact science, it's very difficult to predict how long a stack will take to dry. It also depends on what you mean by 'dry'. Sweeping generalizations such as 'leave it one year per inch of thickness' don't take into account the climatic conditions, the time of year or the species of timber. Species has the greatest influence, with open textured timbers drying far more readily than fine textured ones. Some are more forgiving than others. Yew, for example, can be worked while still quite wet yet remain stable. However, species such as oak must be quite dry.

You can monitor how dry the wood is by using a moisture meter. Although bear in mind that it's impossible to air dry timber in the UK much below 18 per cent. Therefore, even leaving it for several years does not mean that it will get any drier. To further reduce the moisture content and to make it safe for use in a centrally heated atmosphere some other form of drying must be applied.

Kiln drying

The aim of any sort of seasoning is to make the timber more stable; at the same time it also makes it stronger. Strength increases dramatically as the timber dries. Some timbers actually have to be worked when wet, particularly certain Australian species, as they're too hard to be nailed or screwed when dry.

A popular misconception is that kiln-dried timber is 'artificially' dried and is consequently inferior. Yet provided the kilning has been carried out properly, there is absolutely no reason why this should be the case. Kilning should not change any of the working properties of the timber, other than those normally associated with drying. This idea has probably arisen because air-dried timber is not always as dry as kiln-dried and therefore seems more 'workable'. The fact that this increased workability often leads to problems when the wood dries out further is often overlooked.

Early kilns were of the progressive type. They were essentially long tunnels, which became warmer as you moved from one end to the other. Timber was loaded at one end and gradually pushed through as successive loads were added. As the wood progressed along

▶ **A modern
compartment type kiln.**

the kiln the temperature rose and drying gradually
increased. These kilns often relied on natural draught
for air circulation and were relatively uncontrollable,
although there were some forced draught versions.
Due to this lack of control, they were only suitable
for batches of timber which were all the same size
and initial moisture content. They could not be varied
to suit different sorts of load within the same chamber.

The more modern kilns are of the compartment
type consisting of a closed chamber with air artificially
provided by fans. This is by far the most popular kiln
type in operation today, producing a huge percentage
of the world's kiln-dried timber. Although they tend to
be highly expensive, this cost is recouped by the added
value produced with each kiln load.

Benefits

Kiln drying offers several advantages. Firstly, it saves
lots of time. You can often convert and use kiln-dried
timber in a matter of months, sometimes even weeks,
so the investment in timber stock can be kept to a bare
minimum. The equivalent air drying time may be a
number of years.

Secondly, you're not at the mercy of the weather
as you are when air drying. Therefore, you can produce
a uniform and regular supply of dry timber regardless
of the weather. You can also achieve much lower
moisture contents, particularly in temperate climates,

as well as maintaining total control over the final
moisture content (MC). Therefore, you can exactly
tailor the final MC to its eventual use.

Modern kilns operate at temperatures of up to
212°F (100°C), so they require an energy input of
some sort. Oil and gas are expensive, so many mills
now totally integrate their production and use wood
waste as a fuel for the kilns. These high temperatures
harden any resins in softwoods, which helps to prevent
them bleeding out in later use. They also tend to have
a sterilizing effect on the timber, therefore killing any
insect or fungal pests.

Cost

Such is their specialized nature, modern kilns require
a high capital cost as well as a large initial investment.
Reducing the size of the conventional kiln to make
it suitable for the small timber business or even the
home user has rarely been successful. The economy
of scale counts for a lot in this situation, as a small kiln
is almost as expensive as a very large one.

Apart from the actual structure, a lot of the cost
is involved with the working mechanism which mimics
the three controlling factors of air drying. Heaters
control temperature, steam determines the relative
humidity and fans provide the essential air movement.
Vents and an array of sophisticated monitoring devices
complete the installation.

◀ **Sophisticated monitoring devices control temperature and humidity within the kiln.**

Dehumidifier kilns

A cheaper option is a dehumidifier kiln. These work on a different principle and are a distinct possibility for the home user. Originally developed in the 1970s, small dehumidifying kilns have continued to evolve. Due to these continued improvements, there is now a range of small-scale units which are suitable for any size of woodworking operation.

The principle is quite simple. Warm dry air is drawn through the sealed drying chamber, picking up the moisture which is evaporating out of the wood. This then passes over refrigerated coils cooling it to below the dew point so that the water condenses out and runs away to an external drain. Following this, air is passed over heated coils for re-circulation, the forced draught is provided by fans as it would be in a conventional kiln.

The beauty of this process is that it's largely self-generating with regards to heat; it effectively works like a fridge in reverse. The water condensing out releases latent heat which warms up the atmosphere in the kiln so that the air can then hold more moisture. For this to work efficiently the drying chamber must be completely sealed, we don't want to extract water from stray air entering the kiln. The chamber must also be well-insulated as it's important to retain as much heat as possible. The warmer the air, the quicker the drying process will be and also the less extra heat input is needed.

Drying by dehumidification has two main advantages. Firstly, the wood produced is usually high quality with little or no degrade, primarily as the drying conditions are so mild. In addition, this means that different species and different sizes can be mixed in the same kiln load. Secondly, the building and running costs are relatively low.

The downside is that drying times are much longer than with a conventional kiln. It takes a lot to extract down to a low MC, especially as the law of diminishing returns seems to apply when you get below 20 per cent.

Simple kiln

Kilns can be as large or as small as you like, working on the same principle as a domestic dehumidifier. In their simplest form they can be placed in a closed and insulated container along with your timber and with the water being extracted as it's drawn over cold refrigerated coils. Many people use a refrigerated container or even build their own structure from scratch.

Building your own dehumidifying kiln

Requirements

Your first decision concerns the size of the unit. The temptation is to build one that is too big for your ongoing requirements. Many people tend to look at the massive pile of timber they've already accumulated and design one to suit this volume. Unfortunately, this is simply not realistic. It's better to calculate how much timber you will actually use in perhaps two months then make a kiln large enough for this volume of timber. Especially as all kilns work better when they're completely full. Although you might have a backlog at this stage, once you get into the drying cycle the kiln may take some filling. This is perhaps one situation where it's better to think small rather than big. Even if you do outgrow the capacity, it's more flexible to have two small kilns than one large one.

The actual drying chamber must be rigid, airtight, insulated and capable of opening easily for loading and unloading. Over the years, I've built five different kilns and have tried all the options. The problem with most homebuilt kilns is not so much the insulation which is easily constructed using sheets of thick polystyrene, but more with getting them to be airtight, and yet still easy to open. Building the kiln from timber with layers of insulation means that the front may be heavy and awkward to move when you're loading. Getting the doors to seal perfectly may also be difficult. However, the advantage of building your own kiln is that it can be created to fit into any available space.

Recycling

By far the easiest option is to buy a suitable chamber of some sort, such as a redundant shipping container. Yet although these are available ready insulated, they tend to be very large and bulky. They're not particularly

◀ **Build the kiln to take just two or three month's supply of timber.**

The author's kiln made from a
fridge body found in a scrap yard.

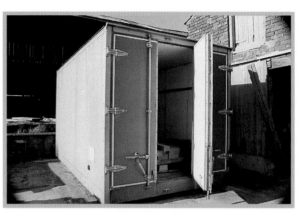

The three doors at the back can be opened
individually or as a whole for loading and unloading.

The hinges and catches
are made from heavy duty
stainless steel.

The original fridge
unit was an ideal location
for the controls.

cheap either. A visit to your local commercial vehicle
scrapyard usually provides something usable. My own
kiln is made from a fridge body I found on the back
of a written off vehicle. The body was intact and had
been used for delivering frozen foods. Consequently,
the insulation was superb. The whole of the inside was
lined, beautifully smooth, and the three doors at the
back could either be opened individually or together
for loading or unloading. There were even lights inside
and the whole thing was totally waterproof!

After a bit of negotiation, I purchased the fridge
for £500 including delivery, which compares very
favourably with the cost of building your own kiln.
The necessary sheets of marine ply as well as all the
insulation would have almost amounted to this price.
I could never have constructed anything as strong with
doors which shut and seal effectively, plus heavy duty
stainless steel hinges and catches.

Having said this, I had to do a fair bit of work
cutting it off the lorry chassis and modifying the back
which originally had walk-in access steps. I also had to
remove the original fridge unit which was mounted on
to the front of the box. This provided an ideal location
for the control panel with the added bonus of a built-in
thermometer. The actual dimensions of the box are:
7in x 6in x 13in (178mm x 152mm x 330mm).

▲ The thermometer was left in place.

▲ The dehumidifier unit
is mounted inside the
drying chamber with a
separate control box outside.   ▼ The drying unit internals.

This is almost too large for my current requirements, however I considered it such a good buy that I was determined to make sure that it worked.

Operation

There are a variety of dehumidifier units available to fit these small kilns, varying from quite tiny to definitely commercial. They consist of the main unit which is mounted inside the drying chamber and a separate control box mounted on the outside unit.

The actual drying unit consists of a compressor unit, refrigerated coils, heat exchanger and a heating coil, with a fan to draw the air over the chilled coils. Water condenses on these coils, then drips into the tray below before running away through a drain hole.

I chose a mid-range model capable of dealing with a variety of load sizes. I wanted to mount the unit at the end of the box, yet I was concerned that the airflow from the dehumidifier alone would not be sufficient. To overcome this problem, I installed an extra fan. Unfortunately, this proved inadequate and I eventually had to add two more. All three fans can be switched on independently to create the necessary airflow.

The skill is in getting the air circulating evenly throughout the stack of timber. This is an almost impossible task, but helped by having as much forced draught as possible. My unit is installed behind a false front at the back of the box. The air is drawn in fairly low down, sucked up through the dehumidifier and then blown out over the top of the stack. A plastic

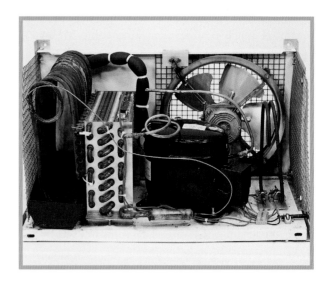

▼ Two more fans were added to increase the air circulation.

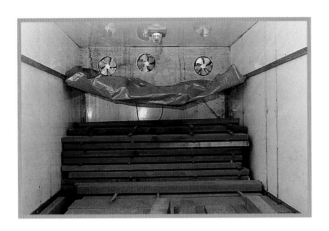

◀ **The kiln in the early stages of filling.**

▶ **Mixing thicknesses can cause cracks in the thickest pieces.**

sheet draped over the top prevents the air from short-circuiting while the extra fans blow it down to the other end of the box ready to be drawn back through the stack. The picture above shows the kiln in the early stages of filling with the sheet rolled out of the way. I've found this works really well, with very minimal variation of moisture content throughout the stack.

Calculations

Your drying unit will come with charts providing guidance on load sizes, operating temperatures and drying times. Although success often comes down to experience – it will take several loads before you feel entirely confident about what you're doing. As a full load of timber is such a major investment, it's worth starting with everything turned down to prevent any serious drying damage. Although this may take longer, at least you will have got a feel for how the kiln works. If you are mixing sizes, always work to the biggest size to avoid moisture gradients which are too steep and may lead to cracks in the wood. For example, if you base your calculations on the smaller section material, the large pieces may crack badly.

In my experience, a full load of around 300ft³ (8.495m³) of hardwood, air-dried to an initial moisture content of 35 per cent, will dry to 10 per cent in about two months on a fairly gentle cycle. The operating temperature seems to stabilize at around 35°F (1.67°C). This heat is mostly generated by the drying process rather than the in-built heaters. In fact, the smaller units don't have additional heaters. Instead they rely purely on self-generated heat.

Drying times vary enormously and depend on the thickness of the material, the initial moisture content, the species and the load size. When my kiln is at full speed, I would expect to fill a 43 pints (25 litre) drum with water every 24 hours initially. It's staggering just how much water there is! Your main control is the length of time the unit is left running for. The timer on the control box switches the unit on or off in 15 minute intervals, simply select how many of these are needed.

The process

The initial start up must be quite slow or the water will freeze on the cooling coils. As the chamber temperature gradually increases, the drier can be left on for longer periods. If the unit is not generating enough heat by itself, the temperature sensor switches the heaters on. Once again, it's better to start with the settings on low and let everything build up slowly.

Loading the kiln is also very important. It's critical that the airflow is not restricted, so stickers should be positioned parallel to the air movement not across it. A small kiln can be loaded in situ, but this is awkward with a larger one. As the stack builds, the boards need to be lifted to the back and there is restricted headroom in the kiln. Consequently, you may need to rig up some sort of rail system which loads the stacks in the doorway, then pushes them into the kiln when they're complete. I build mine on large pallets, then slide them in with a pallet truck.

Once the kiln is full and running, try to avoid the temptation to keep opening it up to see what is happening inside, this is why good temperature monitoring is important. The best way to access this is to monitor the amount of water running out of the kiln. This will progressively increase, then stabilize for a while before quickly tailing off. There is a danger here of 'overcooking' the load, so be vigilant when things start to slow down. You will also have to open the kiln occasionally to check the MC of a few sample boards.

When you've reached the level you're happy with, switch the drier off, but leave the fans running for a couple of days. This allows all the timber to cool and the moisture gradients to even out. Bringing hot wood into a cold atmosphere can cause it to crack.

Drying

Whatever type of kiln is used, it's always advantageous to firstly remove as much of the free water as possible via air drying. This is relatively easy to do and is often almost as quick by air drying as it is in an expensive kiln. A well-organized timber yard will have stacks of timber coming through in succession ready to go into the kiln when their initial moisture level has dropped.

> ## Easy does it!
>
> These small kilns work really well, even if they are rather inaccurate. Their main advantage is that you can tailor one to your exact needs. It's also quite difficult to spoil the wood provided you take it all very gently. Although only building up experience will give you total confidence.

As well as the cost implications, partially air-dried timber always dries with less degrade than freshly sawn timber. Similarly, the thicker the timber the harder it is to kiln, with anything above 3in (76mm) taking a disproportionate length of time. Thick material is therefore uneconomic to kiln, which is why it's rarely available at timber merchants. Softwoods will stand much more drastic conditions than hardwoods, as we would expect taking into account what we now know about their structure.

◄ **Stacks are initially air-dried ready for kilning.**

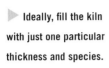
▶ Ideally, fill the kiln with just one particular thickness and species.

▼ Normally only square edged stock is kiln-dried.

Therefore, it's important to fill a kiln with just one particular thickness and species. If they're mixed you will have to work at the schedule for the slowest to be safe. To give an example of time scale, a 1ft (0.30m) oak will dry from green to 10 per cent moisture content

in about five weeks based on a schedule to minimize degrade. This is a relatively long time to tie up your substantial timber investment in an expensive-to-run kiln, therefore it's vital that you get as much timber into the kiln as possible.

Drying waney edged boards is very wasteful, so the usual procedure is to only load square edged stock. However, this means a loss to the continuity of a log with special arrangements having to be made if the boards need to be kept in sequence.

Obviously, if you make a mistake with a full kiln it's likely to be an expensive one, so the drying process has to be very closely monitored according to a detailed schedule. The schedule for each species has been drawn

◀ Timber should be stacked carefully to maintain continuity if the boards need to be kept in sequence.

107

◁ **Poor support will cause the boards to sag and distort.**

final stage of the drying process is a conditioning and equalization phase. This allows the remaining moisture to redistribute itself evenly throughout the timber. It's at this stage that steam can be introduced to correct any case hardening that may have occurred.

In tropical areas, there has also been various experimentation with solar kilns, using the sun to either heat the wood directly or to produce electricity to power heaters. Obviously, such a system is entirely

up according to thickness, initial moisture content and the final intended moisture content. Strict adherence to these is vital, particularly in the early stages when the timber is quite wet. Controlling the relative humidity is also critical for establishing a safe moisture gradient.

Bear in mind

I mentioned the importance of good stickering with reference to air drying, and it's just as important, if not more so, during kilning. Plenty of evenly spaced stickers are essential for flat boards. They also always produce better quality timber, so they're well worth the extra effort. Just look at the effects of poor support, including sagging and distortion, in the picture above. Regardless of how good the monitoring is, there will always be areas which dry quicker than others. So, the

▲ **Solar kilns are sometimes used in tropical areas.**

◁ **Kiln-dried timber re-stacked outside, even undercover will inevitably take up moisture again.**

▶ Imported timber is often tightly wrapped in plastic, which can cause sweating and discolouration.

dependent on there being enough sunshine, so some of your independence is lost. They also have a limited capacity, the relative surface area for a solar collector decreases as the stack gets bigger. I've actually bought and used timber dried by this method in Zimbabwe, yet they continue to have limited commercial success.

Bear in mind that obtaining dry wood is not the end of the process, keeping it at that final moisture content is just as important. Realistically, this probably means keeping it indoors in a heated storage area. Just because it has been dried to perhaps 10 per cent this doesn't mean it will stay at this level.

Storing it outside, even under cover, will soon have the moisture content back up to 15 per cent. A storage area in the workshop fitted with a small domestic dehumidifier is ideal, especially if you're aiming to make furniture that will end up in a centrally heated atmosphere. If this is not possible, it's vital that you bring the timber into a similar environment to its final destination and condition it for a few weeks before use.

Keeping the timber dry in transit is another problem, particularly if it has to travel far. Deliveries of kiln-dried material from your timber merchant should always be well covered to protect it from the elements. Packs of dried timber are often tightly wrapped in plastic, although this can have its own problems with thicker material sweating and subsequently discolouring due to the growth of fungi.

Timber defects

Once it becomes well-known that you work with wood it's surprising just how quickly logs start to appear on your doorstep. Unfortunately, the majority of these logs arrive wet, usually freshly sawn, and a long way off from being anywhere near ready to use.

Just how far away is rarely appreciated by the seasoning beginner. We all set out with great hopes of utilizing vast amounts of cheap timber only to be thwarted at the drying stage. Often you're left wondering whether the effort was really worth it. At best home seasoning is time-consuming, and at worst frustrating and disappointing. What at first

▼ A lot of wasted work is involved for the home user trying to convert round logs into usable timber.

It's possible to produce decorative
objects from seemingly unusable timber.

No half measures

Don't be tricked into thinking that nearly dry
timber is good enough either. It must be dried
to a moisture content that's in total balance
with its surrounding environment or you are
simply wasting your time trying to work it.

So far

What we've learnt so far is that seasoning a piece of
green timber involves the removal of all the free water
and some of the bound water, until the moisture level
is in equilibrium with the surrounding environment.
However, this removal of water must be carefully
controlled to minimize degrade. This term is used
to describe a whole variety of defects that can occur
during seasoning and all of which are a result of
incorrect drying procedures.

It's the words 'carefully controlled' which are key.
You could just stick the wet wood in an oven and drive
off the moisture quite quickly. In fact, I often hear of
people putting large chunks in the airing cupboard to
'speed it up'. All that happens is that the wood dries so
unevenly that huge stresses develop and the resulting
defects totally ruin the timber.

Phases

The drying process is much more controlled with
three distinct phases.

Phase 1

In a freshly sawn board there is uniform moisture
content throughout, well above the fibre saturation
point (FSP). Water immediately starts to evaporate
from the surface and the drying process begins. At
this stage there is no shrinkage, so no stresses or
defects. This can be a very misleading stage providing
you with beautifully flat and defect-free boards, plus
a deceptively good return from the log, but just wait!

appears to be a very inexact procedure is actually
dependant on distinct scientific principles governed
by two abiding and inescapable truths. Firstly, there
are no short cuts, you just have to be patient. Secondly,
wet wood is of no use.

Having said this, it's quite possible to season
your own wood and the thrill of producing a beautiful
object from what was once a soggy wet log lying in
some obscure field is well worth all the heartache.
Yet to achieve this with any consistency, it's essential
to understand the drying process thoroughly. Then
you will use timber only when it's in a proper useable
state and you can fully appreciate the warning signs
and potential pitfalls.

 The flat and clean freshly sawn face deteriorates as the board dries.

Surface checking on freshly sawn beams.

Round logs will also crack on the end when they start to dry.

The surface wood distorts, referred to as collapse.

Phase 2

As the drying continues, the surface water drops below the FSP and the outer layers of the wood begin to shrink. Yet the core remains wet and swollen limiting the amount of shrinkage and causing tension to develop around the edges of the board. If this tension becomes too great, the wood breaks and surface checks develop to relieve it. The same thing happens in round logs.

As this battle continues, the tensioned outer layers begin to compress the wet core. This compression may cause distortion of the core cells, a condition known as collapse and illustrated by the picture on the right. This is rare in home-grown timbers, but tends to be more common among North American timbers and are a regular feature of the Australian Eucalyptus genus.

▼ **The classic case hardening test.**

▶ **Re-sawing stressed boards produces severe distortion.**

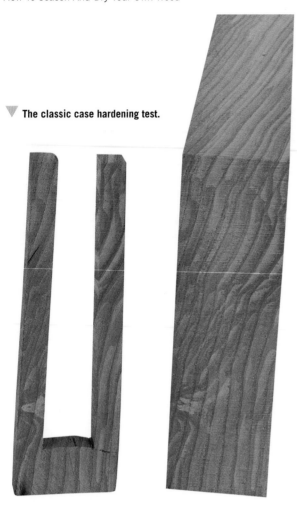

Special drying schedules have been established for susceptible woods, usually involving a long period of air dying prior to kilning. In some cases, it's possible to initiate a reconditioning process to collapsed timber, involving heating it in a water saturated atmosphere for several hours. This usually restores the original condition with the resulting timber having similar strength properties to uncollapsed material with a similar moisture content.

Phase 3

Yet there is another scenario, resulting in a complete reversal of the situation. If the drying process is reasonably well-controlled, the outside dries and tries to shrink as above, but the developing tensions are not enough to cause splitting. The outside fully dries and sets to its finished size. Yet the core dries more slowly, eventually dropping below the FSP and shrinking.

However the core is now restrained by the outer surface and therefore ends up in tension, pulling the outer layer into compression. This is the classic condition of case hardening and may explain a phenomenon you have witnessed, yet never previously understood. With the outer layers now in compression, any surface checks which developed earlier on now close up and to all intents disappear. Yet they are still there and will reappear if you cut the wood in such a way that the compression is released. Wood cannot heal itself. Case hardening should therefore not be confused with the engineering term of the same name, which implies greater hardness.

You can test for this by cutting a cross section in the board, sawing this into two prongs as shown in the picture above, then allowing them to stand in a warm atmosphere for 24 hours. If there is case hardening the prongs will bend inwards, sometimes dramatically.

Case hardening can be removed by steaming the timber to replace water in the outer layers. If this is done soon enough and the wood is then re-dried again properly, the resulting timber is quite sound and is in no way inferior. As the drying continues, the wood reaches uniform moisture content, but remains stressed. Any attempts to resaw the boards produces severe distortion.

Occasionally, these stresses are so severe that the tissues break up, a defect referred to as honeycombing. This causes major internal damage which may or may not be visible on the surface. Honeycombing usually only occurs along the rays in tangentially sawn boards of hardwood. It rarely occurs in air-dried material because the conditions are not harsh enough.

Additional defects

Hopefully, you can now begin to appreciate the whole dilemma involved with any form of seasoning. Water only moves from a wet area to a drier one, so in order to begin seasoning you must develop a moisture gradient through the timber. However, this is exactly what causes the differential shrinkage and stresses. To prevent this from happening, the gradient must be kept as shallow as possible, but then the moisture will only move very slowly!

In order to balance the speed of drying against the likely outcome with regard to defects, we have to reach a compromise. Ideally, we would establish a moisture gradient specific to each piece of wood we're attempting to dry. However, if you're trying to dry a whole batch of timber this is impossible. The picture below shows two pieces of beefwood within the same kiln load. Although they were both dried under identical conditions, the thicker piece has cracked badly because its dimensions are such that the moisture gradient within the timber is very different to that of the thinner piece. Although the gradient was fine for the thinner one, it was too steep for the thicker piece.

End grain splitting during drying is another problem that is difficult to avoid. Some species are more prone to it than others. Beech, for example, is particularly affected. Before the widespread use of liquid end sealers, the classic approach was to nail a cleat across the end of the board to restrain the splitting influence. Yet these are rarely helpful and even tend to exacerbate the problem as the longitudinal shrinkage of the cleat is far less than the radial or tangential shrinkage of the board. This generates its own tension and subsequent cracking. Similar problems occur with the metal ties used to hold exotic logs together until sawing, again often generating more problems than they actually solve.

Establishing a moisture gradient
suitable for the thickness of the timber
is important to minimize cracking.

Cleats nailed across the end of boards to prevent splitting are rarely successful.

It's important to recognize that not all defects are seasoning related. Jagged, random cracks, particularly in the end grain, usually result from poor felling or crosscutting where the butt has broken off rather than being cut cleanly. Such cracks often travel a long way up the butt and can lead to lot of wastage at the conversion stage.

So called 'thunder shakes' are also caused by poor felling. If one log is dropped across another the sudden shock impact causes lots of internal cracking, which becomes more apparent as the log dries. This should not be confused with the condition of brittleheart. Although it's symptoms are similar, brittleheart develops when adjacent areas of different anatomical structure, usually reaction wood, shrink differently relative to each other. These are natural compression failures rather than man-made.

Bigger problems occur when the shrinkage is uneven throughout the board, causing it to end up distinctly out of shape. This is known as 'warp'.

Metal ties are often used to prevent exotic logs splitting too severely.

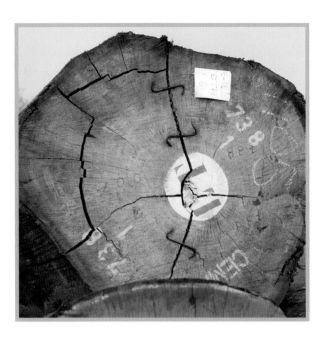

The cracks on jagged ends are usually the result of poor felling.

Thunder shakes are usually caused by felling one log across another.

Its many different types may or may not be permanent. Where shrinkage generates stresses which are not released by one of the forms of warp, rupture of the tissues occurs resulting in splits, checks and shakes. These are usually visible externally on the ends or the face of a board, but may also be internal.

Warp

There is a range of other timber defects brought about by drying, but I shall start by looking at the various forms of warp:

'Twist' occurs when all four corners of the dried board do not lie on the same plane. This is one of the most serious defects often rendering the board totally useless. Twist is usually the result of spiral or interlocked grain, but can sometimes be generated by the uneven shrinkage of a board containing wood of varying densities. You can minimize the problem by taking care with the stacking and by using plenty of stickers immediately after cutting the wood. Yet you can't really control it and it's virtually impossible to put right once the timber is dry.

Twist is virtually impossible to correct once the timber is dry.

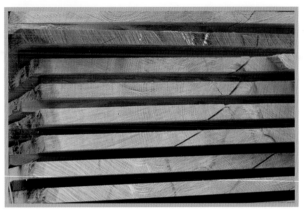

◁ **Warping across
the width of the board
is termed as 'cupping'.**

▽ **Truly quarter-sawn
material is more stable,
decorative and expensive.**

'Cupping' refers to warping across the width of the board. Most through and through cut boards have one surface more radial than the other. As radial shrinkage is less than tangential, the face towards the centre of the tree tends to shrink less and the board cups away from the centre. This is why truly quarter-sawn material is so stable and desirable. If you want to use it at full thickness, cupped timber has to be cut into narrower widths, therefore creating wide boards can be very wasteful.

'Bowing' is similar to cupping, but tends to occur along the length of the board rather than across its width. This is usually a result of the planks being stacked and sticked badly during drying, rather than any physiological cause. Again this causes a lot of waste, particularly if you are cutting out long lengths. So always start your cutting out process with the longer lengths from the flatter boards and leave the short ones to be cut from the more bowed boards.

◁ **Bowing is normally
caused by bad stacking.**

▶ **Spring: massive internal stresses released as the board dries.**

'Spring' or 'crook' is when the board bends along the longitudinal plane, yet still remains flat. It results from massive internal stresses being released as the log is sawn. Spring is more common in timber taken from the centre of the tree or in particular species such as beech. Fortunately it's not too wasteful, unless again you need long lengths.

'Kink' is a localized spring, usually due to a knot on the edge of a board setting up differential shrinkage. It can occur in any timber, yet like spring it doesn't cause lots of problems, despite some potential localized cracking around the knot.

Further terminology

It's also important at this stage to define the varied, yet commonly confused terms 'check', 'split' and 'shake'. These are all ruptures of the actual wood tissues in a longitudinal plane.

Checks and splits

'Checks' form when uneven shrinkage generates a stress greater than the inherent strength of the wood and separation of cells occurs along the grain. These separations usually occur only on the surface of the wood. If, as they do on occasion, they extend right through the board from face to face, they're

▼ **Large knots on the edge of the board may cause it to kink.**

▶ **Checks occur on the surface, but are rarely very deep.**

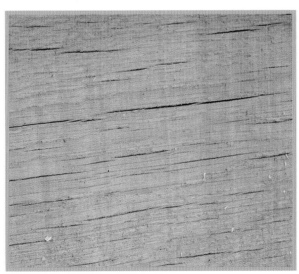

◁ Splits extend through the board.

▷ Overheating during sanding can generate fine end grain checks.

referred to as 'splits'. Both checks and splits may close up if the dry timber later becomes damp. However, once the damage is done they're always present even if they're invisible. Dry timber doesn't have the capacity to heal itself.

You can generate checks by heavy sanding, particularly on the lathe. If you're using fine grained woods like yew or box, and the timber has become too hot with all the frictional heat, simply stop and

look closely at the surface, particularly the end grain. This will probably appear fine, but when you put on a coat of sealer a mass of fine checks will appear, looking like tiny white lines. These are entirely the result of over-heating during sanding, so take care.

◁ Ring shakes are cracks that follow the growth ring.

▽ Star shakes radiate outwards from the centre often following the ray tissue.

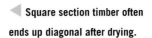

Square section timber often ends up diagonal after drying.

Shakes

Serious splits are called 'shakes' and usually refer to defects in the log, not always due to drying stresses. They are more likely to be the result of in-built growth stresses which are released as the tree is felled. Shakes may be in the form of a ring shake where the separation of tissues follows a growth ring, as in the log of *Lignum vitae* in the picture below left. They may also take the form of a star shake which radiates outwards from the centre, often following ray tissue.

Shrinkage

Square section timber with growth rings orientated at an angle will shrink far more across one diagonal than the other. This pulls the square into a distinct diamond shape, as shown in the picture top left. We can see the equivalent to this in a piece of turning with the greater tangential shrinkage converting this rough-turned round into an oval. The difference between tangential and radial shrinkage is illustrated perfectly by the picture on the left. The tangential shrinkage at the right hand edge of the board has left the thickness noticeably less than the radial shrinkage on the left.

Variations in the shrinkage rates can occur within the same board.

Tangential shrinkage turns rough turned bowls significantly oval.

Choose carefully

Species with low tangential to radial shrinkage percentages are obviously a far better bet to attempt to dry in the round. For example, species such as yew and lime rarely crack significantly on the end, yet box wood will usually split along the length of the log.

◀ **Radial cracking is common in small logs.**

If you've ever tried to season your own logs you will probably have come across the most frustrating example of shrinkage, 'radial cracking'. This is caused by the remaining mass of the log being unable to accommodate the stress generated by tangential shrinkage. There is nowhere for the distortion to go, so the log starts to split down its length.

Rough turning when wet can help to minimize shrinkage, but it does not eradicate it completely. The two laburnum logs shown in the picture below, for example, both succumbed only six months after turning. These pieces illustrate a very interesting point in that the cracks both developed from a point of weakness. The one on the right evolved from the heart of a knot where a branch joined the main trunk. While the one on the left developed around a hole I created when pulling a nail out during rough turning.

This radial cracking should not be confused with end checking, caused by uneven drying. Water moves much more quickly longitudinally along the grain than it does across it. Consequently, end grain loses its moisture more quickly than the inside of the board. As it drops below the FSP it starts to shrink, resulting in the characteristic end checking. However, this is usually not serious and by removing a small end slice you will reveal a clean surface. Coating the end grain

▼ **Rough turning wet logs to minimize shrinkage can help, but is not always successful.**

▼ **End checking is caused by uneven drying.**

drying, that there must be differential drying to make the water move out, although the moisture gradient between the wet and dry areas must not be too steep or cracking will develop. End sealing and natural bark are two coatings which help to reduce this gradient.

Variation

Sometimes shrinkage properties vary even within the same piece of wood, this is usually caused by the reaction wood we looked at earlier. This wood tends to shrink far more longitudinally than usual. Normal wood has a restraining effect, while reaction wood splits across the axis of the grain. The variation of density in spalted wood often causes the shrinkage rates to vary accordingly, leading to checks along the lines of the fungal zones.

The presence of extractives can also seriously affect the shrinkage properties of a board. The boundary between the heartwood and sapwood is therefore often found to be a trouble spot. The differential shrinkage in some of the exotic timbers is sometimes so great that the two actually separate as the timber dries. In home-grown timbers, I've noticed that a depression frequently forms right on the boundary.

of wet boards and logs with a sealer of some sort will go a long way towards slowing down this rapid end drying, but it's difficult to eliminate it entirely.

Drying through the edge of a board or a log is slower and more controlled. Taking the bark off to hasten the drying process also has it merits, as shown in the pictures below. Both pictures are of the same Amazon rosewood log, one with the bark left on and the other with it removed. The debarked side shows deep radial cracks and surface checks, but the side with the bark still intact shows very little degrade. This illustrates one of the guiding principles of timber

◀▼ Leaving the bark on a log slows the rate of drying through the side and lessens checking.

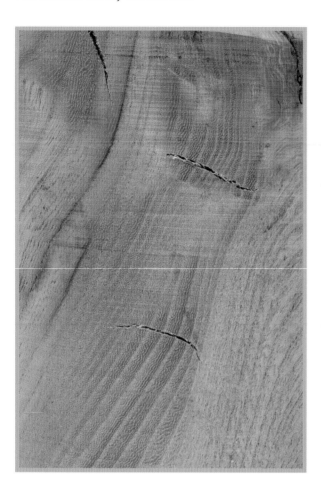

◁ Reaction wood
will often crack across
the axis of the grain.

▽ The heartwood and
sapwood may separate
during drying if the differential
shrinkage is too great.

Working with logs and home seasoning

With the ever-increasing price of timber, newcomers to woodworking can often be a little hesitant due to the ongoing cost of suitable wood. However, there is actually a lot of very usable material available in the form of small branches and garden prunings. Many of these are highly decorative species and what's more are often free for the taking, although check first. This wood is probably mostly of interest to woodturners and carvers as it's ideal for a whole range of small projects like lamps, goblets, eggcups and boxes. Some of the bigger logs can also be cut down into small planks for box making and the like. This allows you to remove the very heart of the tree, the area which generates all of the problems when seasoning in the round.

Of course there is a downside to all this free bounty. The biggest snag is that you cannot use it in its raw state. It has to be seasoned properly before it's turned. Unfortunately, trying to season logs is usually even more unpredictable than seasoning sawn timber. Also it's more often than not very disappointing as it always seems to crack and degrade. The only consolation is that there is very little cost involved, your only investment being the time involved in moving and storing the wood.

Key

Storage and time are the two key parameters for successful home seasoning. Unfortunately, there are no short cuts. Attempting to speed up the drying process always ends in failure, or rather even more failure than usual. Although experience will soon help you to build up knowledge of those species that season well and those that don't.

▶ Small branches pruned from garden trees and used in the round can provide interesting timber.

The biggest enemy to successful drying is extremes of temperature, so store the wood away from direct sunlight. Ideally, leave it in a cool, airy shed with plenty of through draught. Failing this, a shaded pile at the bottom of the garden will suffice. Rain isn't really a problem.

Remember that it will take several years to dry, so pile it up, then simply forget about it. Although always leave the bark on to minimize differential shrinkage. For 3–4in (76–102mm) diameter material, for example, I'd expect to leave it at least a couple of years for the initial drying. Be wary of putting the wood in the loft or the garage roof as the heat built up here during the summer can be tremendous and will spoil the timber within hours.

Next steps

After a couple of years of this slow and stable outside drying, I cut the logs into manageable lengths, then stack them underneath the lathe bench. The heated workshop is maintained at a constant temperature, so never gets excessively hot. Check the pile occasionally

▼ Cut timber must be stored out of direct sunlight.

Patience

As the smaller logs are used in the round, there is effectively quite a thickness of timber to be dried out, therefore much patience is required. If you are not of that disposition, buy yourself some ready dried blanks and save yourself the frustration.

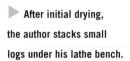
After initial drying, the author stacks small logs under his lathe bench.

to see how things are going and to make sure there is no worm infestation, particularly in the sapwood of species like oak or cherry.

Following another couple of years, I would expect the branches to be nearly dry, especially as the relative humidity in the workshop is quite low. Yet just because they have been stored for quite a few years, doesn't necessarily mean that they will be dry. Wood is like a sponge and will take up moisture as well as lose it if the conditions are damp. When the surrounding atmosphere is damp, the wood could be there for 50 years and still not dry out.

Even after my relatively controlled drying, there will still be some serious radial cracking and checking on the end of the logs, which often goes quite deep. Cutting off successive slices to remove these cracks wastes a lot of material. Species like laburnum, for example, are very prone to degradation and can lose 4–5in (102–127mm) on the end of each log. Sealing the ends with paint or wax will reduce this splitting, but rarely eliminates it.

Even more damaging are the longitudinal cracks that effectively split the log into two. These are almost inevitable in very fine-grained species such as box or

Drying splits will often lead to the loss of several inches off the end of each log.

◀ **Very fine grained species develop longitudinal cracks down their whole length.**

Successfully seasoned branches can be very decorative particularly if you capitalize on the distinctive effects of a heartwood and sapwood mixture. The ratio of these two sections varies tremendously even within the same tree, yew is a wonderful example.

Size

If you try to season bigger logs the problems become even greater. With much more material involved both the drying time and the moisture gradients across the diameter are extended. Even if these gradients don't cause as much cracking as you would find on smaller logs, they generally lead to drying stresses building up within. Subsequent attempts to turn this apparently sound log, ends up with crack appearing either as you use it or after the job is finished.

lilac, unless you control the drying minutely. They are also always exacerbated by removing the bark, as the drying becomes far too rapid. Burying these logs in wet sand so they can dry out really slowly is the only way I've found to minimize these longitudinal cracks.

Don't confuse this end checking with the star shake often found in timbers like walnut and yew shown in the picture below. This defect can be seen throughout the whole tree and is specially disfiguring, but has nothing to do with the seasoning.

▼ **Internal star shakes are a natural feature of some species and are nothing to do with drying.**

▶ **The distinctive contrast between hardwood and sapwood is often very decorative.**

Birch soon rots so it needs to be used quickly.

Ornamental species such as cherry, are usually more decorative once converted.

However, these mid-sized logs can again yield some fabulous timber. A little time spent with a chainsaw often pays dividends, even with the scrappiest looking logs. As they're so much bigger they obviously take much longer to dry evenly. Also, select the species of wood carefully. Birch can be a very attractive timber, but if left piled up for too long it soon starts to rot. This is one species that has to be turned when it's still slightly wet in order to keep it sound. If you do leave it too long the characteristic yellow spalting soon appears and the timber soon becomes unusable. Unfortunately, this rotting is internal and is therefore not always so evident from the outer end of the log. Cutting through the log is the only way to see what's going on.

Figure

A good look at the outside can often tell you a lot about the likely internal figuring. While some perfectly straight and almost cylindrical branches of ash may look encouraging, the interior timber will show very little in the way of figure. Instead it may well be plain and straight grained with the evenness of the annual rings showing up in a very regular pattern.

More ornamental species, like cherry, are much more likely to provide figure. Yet in some gardens even this can grow quite rapidly, resulting in very plain and rather boring timber. Look for logs with natural features which cause a disturbance to the

regular pattern of growth. Cherry tree branches often grow out in regular rings. Cutting through this part can yield some wonderful figuring, even if it doesn't appear so from the outside. Most of the fruitwoods are good. Damson, in particular, is highly decorative with pinky red streaks running through the heartwood.

Yew from logs with a straight smooth bark is renowned for being very sound and shake free, but it's equally plain and uninteresting. Logs with masses of tiny branches have much more potential as these show up as tiny, wonderfully colourful, burr patterns with red and purple markings. Even better, a crotch area where

Timber from straight cylindrical branches are usually plain and straight grained with very little figure.

▼ Features that cause a disturbance to regular growth pattern can result in decorative figuring.

▲ Lots of tiny side branches growing out from species such as yew produce wonderfully colourful markings.

two branches join always produces very decorative ripple effects, equal to some of the most expensive exotic timbers. You don't have to spend a fortune to obtain really good looking wood.

A good-sized bandsaw is needed to get the most out of these logs and to reveal what's going on within. Further careful cutting reduces some of the irregularities and turns your piece of firewood into something usable. In this case, I have cut through the yew crotch and trimmed one half into a turning blank from which I hope to make a large vase.

As with any log you're never quite sure what you will get until it's actually turned. This is particularly true when the bark is so fluted and the centres have to be positioned carefully to yield the maximum possible diameter at each end.

▼ Careful trimming can turn a piece of plywood into usable timber.

▼ Cuts through the crotch area where two branches join can create very decorative ripple effects.

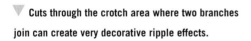

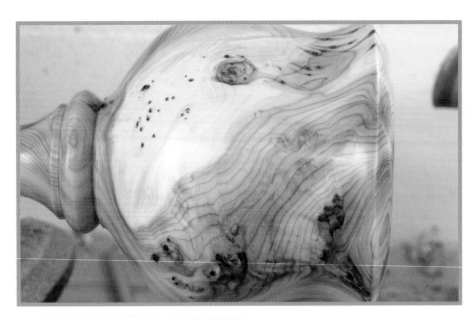

The resulting swirl effect.

Roughing it

If you're a woodturner or a carver you could consider rough turning the green logs into approximate shapes to reduce the thickness and leave you with less material to dry.

Practical application

This particular one turned out successfully, but it's interesting to note the difference in figure between the two sides of the blank. Remember that it was cut from a crotch, so the outer side shows the typical nicely marked, but not outstanding yew patterns. The side which was inside the crotch is much more interesting showing some fantastic swirl effects. Take care with these divided branches though, as there can sometimes be a very large internal bark inclusion down the join which renders them totally useless.

Alternatively, when working with these larger branches try to convert them into boards using the bandsaw, as shown in Chapter 3. This will obviously speed up the drying process as the sections are then much thinner. However, deep cutting like this is notoriously tricky, as well as being heavy on blades, so it may not be a viable alternative if a lot of timber is involved.

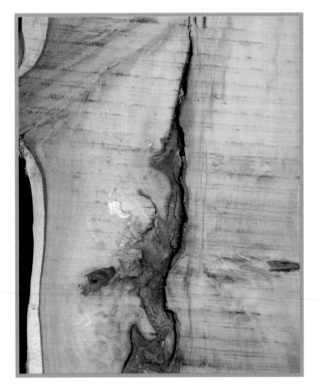

Large internal bark inclusions often ruin crotch pieces.

▶ **Most freshly cut logs will crack immediately after cutting.**

Rough turning for lathe blanks

The term 'rough turning' refers to the process of turning pieces of wet timber to something near their finished size in order to shorten their drying time. This is usually when making bowls, but you can also rough turn other sections. Consequently, you are only drying the material you actually need rather than a lot of additional waste.

Timber with a high moisture content is of little use for normal work as it frequently shrinks, cracks and distorts, as well as being very difficult to finish. The moisture level needs to be reduced to about 8–10 per cent if it's to be dimensionally stable in a modern centrally heated environment. Unfortunately, drying to this level will take a considerable amount of time, often many years, particularly when using the commonly chunky woodturning blanks.

The old adage is that you need a year to dry for every inch of thickness. For example, a 4in (102mm) bowl blank will take at least four years to dry. While this is not strictly true, it gives an idea of the necessary time. There is lots more to it than this and a lot of scientific intricacies involved. Suffice to say that anything you can do to speed up the drying process is very useful, particularly with regard to the thicker sections required by woodturners.

Procedure

Rough turning has proved its worth time and time again. Basically it involves removing as much of the unwanted material as possible, yet leaving enough for truing up after the item has finished distorting during drying. With large bowls this means leaving a wall thickness of about 1in (25mm) all over. Therefore a 4in (100mm) thick blank for example, which would usually take 4 years to dry would become 1in (25mm) thick and then only takes 12 months to dry.

Smaller diameter work can be left even thinner, yet to some extent this varies with the species of timber. With more experience you will come to know which species warp the most. Fine textured species are often more difficult to dry successfully than coarser wood, like ash.

Working with wet timber inevitably generates a large amount of waste. Some bowls crack completely while others distort too far to be of any use. There is often no obvious reason why some fail and others don't. The only consolation is the time saved with the ones that do work and the knowledge that your original wet timber was probably very inexpensive, therefore you've only lost labour input.

Practical application

To illustrate this concept, I'm using some cherry logs left lying around for about 12 months but were still nowhere near dry enough to use. These logs are all of fairly uniform size at about 9in (22.9cm) diameter. This is not a particularly useful size as it means they're slightly too large to turn in the round, but too small to cut into planks. However, it's the size often produced by ornamental garden type trees, so you have to make the most of it. Even freshly cut logs kept outside in a cold winter atmosphere like this soon crack at the ends, so the quicker you start working on them the better.

At this stage, you have to decide exactly what you want to make out of the timber and cut it accordingly. I used one of the logs to cut material for some heavy lamp bases, some natural edged bowls, some normal bowls and finally some dimension stock.

For the lamps, it's simply a question of crosscutting sections out of the log with a chainsaw, making them more or less the finished length of the lamp. These

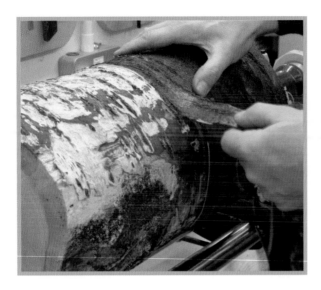

Remove any loose bark before you start.

Sapwood will have often decayed so needs to be removed.

particular trees had obviously grown with a lot of in-built stress as the minute I began to cut them they started to crack in an effort to relieve those stresses, not a good sign for successful conversion.

Firstly, remove anything that's very loose, then find a comfortable speed and start to rough the bark off the log. Take care as the bark can peel off in long strips or lumps that can fly off or give you a nasty whack on your hand.

The bark often contains lots of grit and is very abrasive, so you will need to sharpen the gouge fairly regularly and also ensure that you're wearing eye protection. Remove all the sapwood if it has already started to rot.

Roughing out the shape is great fun. The wet timber simply peels away in a continuous ribbon which piles up on the floor. You will get very wet though as the spray goes everywhere, so wedge up a board at the back of the lathe to take the worst of it. The turned shape only needs to very approximate. Take away as much timber as possible while still leaving enough to put in the detail after drying.

To further relieve the internal stresses and to speed up the drying, I also bore the lamp blanks through at this stage which ensured the centre of the blank dried more evenly. As we've already seen, it's the evenness of drying that's key. When it's very uneven, the resulting differential shrinkage will cause all sorts of cracking

Wet timber peels away in continuous ribbons.

Blanks for turning lamps should be bored through to help equalize drying stresses.

◄ Brush a sealer onto the end grain areas.

▼ Weigh the blank regularly to keep track of the moisture loss.

problems. The other aid to even drying is to seal all the areas of end grain with something impermeable. I use proprietary End Seal, an emulsified wax you simply brush on. You can also use hot paraffin wax if you have the facility. Be liberal with the sealer as it minimizes all the end cracking, although even this will not eliminate it entirely.

Once it's all sealed, write the weight on the blank to help you keep track of the moisture loss over the next few months. Regular weighing will highlight just how much water is being lost. When it becomes constant the blank will be as dry as it will get in that particular atmosphere.

Bowls

To make the natural edged bowls simply split a log through the middle or, if it's big enough, either side of the middle to remove the very heart of the wood. Cracking always seems to originate at the central pith, so anything that removes this will again minimize the risk of splits. Stand the logs on end on the bandsaw

table to cut them through, having first crosscut them with a chainsaw. Never attempt to crosscut logs on the bandsaw as they will snatch and roll dangerously. Once the blank has one full flat, it's safer to control on the bandsaw. You can leave them like this if you wish, but I prefer to cut them roughly into a disc to eliminate as much waste as possible. Seal the ends thoroughly as before.

▶ Blanks for natural edged bowls are best cut to size to minimize the waste that has to be dried.

◀ **Logs should be restrained
on a jig for the initial slicing.**

For conventional bowl blanks, cut the logs into mini boards. The best way to do this is to slice through the middle of the log while it's safely bolted to a sled jig. This consists of two pieces of timber screwed together at right angles. Wet logs cut really easily. It's best to use a ½in (13mm) x3 skip blade in the bandsaw, but remember the push stick for additional safety.

Next, mark out the blanks on the plank and cut them in the normal way. Be careful not to cut right up to the end of the log. Even if they're not obvious, the ends will have some quite deep splits in which

only become apparent as you cut out the blanks. These take some removing and you will have to cut back several inches to get clear of them.

The rough turning process for a bowl is just like any other form of bowl turning. Try to get the wall thickness and the base to an even thickness of around 1in (25mm). Then seal the end grain areas of the turned bowls, as well as the spindle blanks. After a year or so, the weight should start to stabilize. This indicates that the timber is drying and you can begin finishing the turning.

▶ **Once you have a
flat surface, the blanks
can then be marked out.**

◀ **Round blanks will typically end up oval.**

A bowl will typically go oval, although this varies with the species. For example, a 12in (30.5mm) bowl will end up 11in (27.9mm) across the width. This is why it's important to leave plenty of thickness. Rough turned bowls will often distort considerably, but with such a thick wall thickness you should be able to true them up to achieve the finished bowl.

Dimension stock

For wet dimension stock, cut out the square sections you need on the bandsaw, leaving them well oversize as they will often distort quite dramatically. Being full thickness means that they will take some time to dry thoroughly.

▶ **Check your stock regularly for insect attacks.**

◀ **The top shelf of the author's timber rack is an ideal drying location.**

Avoid bringing the rough turnings into a warm atmosphere straight away or they will start to split. I leave mine to acclimatize in a cool atmosphere for at least a couple of months before bringing them into the warmth of the workshop to completely finish drying. The top shelf of my timber rack is ideal for storing the timber for 12 months or more. Although remember to inspect them regularly. Species such as cherry are very vulnerable to attack by worms. Dispose of any blanks which show any traces of pests. You can also speed up the process at this point by putting the rough turned blanks into a dehumidifying type kiln, reducing the complete cycle to a matter of months.

That's all there is to rough turning. It's great fun, but also often very frustrating. As soon as you've finished, clear up the huge pile of wet shavings before wiping the tools and the lathe down with an oily rag to remove the moisture. The sap can be very corrosive and will quickly spoil any bare metal surfaces.

Microwave seasoning

Although I'm familiar with most of the methods for seasoning timber, the use of a microwave oven to speed up the process of drying turned pieces is relatively new to me. I'm therefore in the early stages of what looks like a very steep learning curve. The main problem is that, as with timber drying in general, the application is a very inexact science, despite well-established scientific principles.

There are so many variables that can potentially affect the outcome that it's very much a 'suck it and see' process. Based on the large amount of literature and internet newsgroups on the subject, microwave seasoning is well-documented. However, everyone appears to have their own individual method, many of which seem to conflict. I'm slowly developing my own technique from scratch, accepting some wastage of timber along the way. So far it appears that virtually all woods can be dried this way, even from very wet.

Having said this, all the schools of thought agree that the thinner and more even the thickness of the timber the better the result. This is logical if you think about it in terms of the moisture gradient throughout the timber and the differential stresses this generates if the section varies enormously.

Practical application

So far I've only experimented with bowls, but this immediately raises another dilemma. Should you turn the bowls to final thickness, then microwave them and accept any distortion as part of the course? Or should you rough turn them, then try to dry them in the microwave, before finishing the turning? The problem with this latter option is that the walls are so much thicker, so the drying gradients are really steep and degrade is much more likely. Generally, I've had more success turning them to the finished size from wet, then drying them. Provided you are patient, the distortion is

A log showing what looks like ripple figure.

Stand the logs on end for cutting on the bandsaw.

not usually too extreme. You should also be able to put them back on the lathe in order to complete any final finishing.

Technique

The species of timber, as well as factors such as initial moisture content and grain orientation, can create significant differences. I have outlined my own technique, but this is not meant to be a definitive guide, instead be prepared to follow your own instincts.

1 Crosscut a length of wet log, long enough to lose any end splits when you cut the blank.

2 Standing the log on end on the bandsaw table, slice down the middle, clear of the central pith. A quick moisture content check will show that it's approaching 30 per cent, far too high for immediate use.

3 Turn your bowl in the normal way, rechecking both the inside and the outside. The inside is a simple hollowing out job. As it's so wet the timber will simply pour out in long streamers, although keep the gouge really sharp for an ultra clean cut. The interior wood turns really easily, but use a pair of callipers to check the wall thickness. I discovered that the more even this thickness, the smaller the distortion after drying.

Turning the wet bowl in the normal way means that it's very easy to cut.

◀ **Check wall thickness using calipers.**

▼ **Weigh the bowl before you start microwaving.**

At this stage, I noticed a small crack radiating from the centre of the blank. This would have been an end split in the original log. I simply hadn't allowed enough length to clear it when I started to crosscut the log. This is a good lesson in not being too greedy. Allowing plenty of room clear of the ends before marking your blanks is often less wasteful in the long run.

4 Next, weigh your bowl; in this case it's about 10oz (280g). This is important as it means you can monitor the drying process. You will need to repeat this process as the drying proceeds.

5 For the actual drying, I use a redundant but still functioning domestic microwave in my workshop. Yet the process makes no mess and very little smell, so you should be safe using your kitchen one.

Put the bowl in the right way up for the first session. Start with a one minute blast on the defrost setting, then open the door to allow the bowl to cool. It will continue crackling and fizzing long after it has come out of the microwave, so let it stand for at least 30 minutes. Following this, place the bowl back in the other way up for another minute on defrost. After four sessions of microwaving and standing, two hours

▶ **Start with the bowl the right way up.**

136

◀ Turn the bowl over
for the second burst.

▼ Keep microwaving until
there is no more weight loss.

in all, leave it overnight to fully stabilize. Although at this stage any distortion of the bowl will be surprisingly minimal.

6 The next day, re-weigh the bowl; in this case it's now down to just over 7oz (200g), then repeat the four blasts at defrost setting for a minute each, by then there should be no further weight loss. Assuming that the timber is now bone dry, a quick calculation is required in order to check the original moisture content:

$$\frac{\text{Weight of water in bowl}}{\text{Dry weight of bowl}} \times 100$$

For this bowl:

$$\frac{300 - 200}{200} \times 100 = 50 \text{ per cent}$$

In this case, the result tallies with what the meter originally indicated.

Using a meter in the dry bowl shows that the actual moisture content is now about 10 per cent. This does not quite tally with the above calculation

▶ **Polyethylene glycol-1000 (PEG) is the most efficient of these stabilizers.**

which assumes that the bowl is totally dry. In these situations, I always question the accuracy of the meter. The bowl is certainly dry enough to be stable. There is also very little shape distortion – only a tiny split which has now opened up. This may close up as the bowl settles down, but I'm convinced that if I'd cut this out before I turned the bowl it would not have occurred. It was not caused by the microwave.

Once the timber is dry, sand and finish it in the conventional way. The effect of cutting when wet should have already left a very fine surface. Inevitably the bowl will not run true, so spin the lathe at a slow speed for all the subsequent finishing operations.

This is very much an ongoing experiment and I still have a lot to learn. My only definite conclusion so far is that it works, as long as you are gentle and expect the odd failure. Short bursts at low power appear to work best. Blasting at full power will cause the bowl to distort and split excessively, so be patient and leave time between each session to allow the timber to stabilize; 30 minutes may seem a long time, but it's far shorter than the years it would take to dry the wood by conventional means.

Seasoning wood with PEG

Alternative methods of wood seasoning involve using chemicals to replace the moisture in the wood and to stabilize it. Many of these chemicals were originally developed for American rifle makers looking for

Caution

Above all, consider safety. You are effectively boiling water in an enclosed vessel, so think carefully about what you are doing at each stage and take extra care.

completely stable walnut blocks suitable for gunstocks. Polyethylene glycol-1000 (PEG) is the most efficient of these stabilizers, providing a safe and easy means of seasoning, especially for part turned wood blanks.

PEG is a waxy, almost white material with the appearance of paraffin wax. It's very soluble, dissolving in water at around 100°F (37.8°C). It's also a by-product of the oil industry and should not be confused with glycol or antifreeze. The beauty of PEG is that it's considered totally safe and is often used in a range of pharmaceuticals and beauty cosmetics. There is no specialized or expensive equipment required and the process is rapid compared to the more conventional methods. The only requirement is that the wood is soaked in a mixture of water and PEG.

Unfortunately, handling the solutions is not very pleasant. They are also expensive to produce with a large amount required even for a small amount of timber. Additionally, PEG restricts the type of polish which can be used on the finished item, as many polishes will not take over the impregnated surface. Its limitations should therefore be weighed against

the merits of having fully stabilized timber. Having said this, PEG might just be the solution for a piece of special or difficult timber.

The process

When green timber is totally immersed in a bath of PEG solution, the PEG molecules replace the water molecules in the cell walls. The wood is then dried, but the PEG molecules remain in place to maintain the swollen state and to ensure that there is no shrinkage or degrade. Obviously, to work effectively the PEG must penetrate throughout the timber, diffusing through the free water of the cells to be

deposited in the walls. The wood must therefore be freshly sawn, or at least have a moisture content that's above the FSP.

When treated with PEG, only about 60 per cent of wood whose moisture content is around the 30 per cent mark will show reduced shrinkage, compared to nearly 100 per cent of wood treated at 100 per cent moisture content.

This solution has been used very successfully by marine archaeologists to stabilize timber which has lain sodden for hundreds of years, the classic example being the wreck of the Mary Rose.

Grain orientation is another key factor determining the effectiveness of PEG. As with all other moisture movements, PEG penetrates far better along the grain than across it. Surface penetration on a radial or tangential surface, for example, is only about 1in (25mm). This is another clue to the effective use of PEG in turning. Roughly shaping objects first to reduce the amount of wood to be treated and to increase the penetration will make the whole process much more efficient. As PEG minimizes shrinkage, there's no need to leave the walls of your rough turnings

▶ Bowl blanks need to be immersed for several weeks.

Treaty blanks are normally air-dried, a process that can be sped up with an oven.

Treated surfaces soon develop surface moulds.

as thick as you would if they were to be naturally dried. Therefore, on an average bowl you only need to skim off about ¼in (6mm).

Some species react better to PEG than others; the greater the density the less successful the treatment. Timbers which are full of resin or other extractives may resist PEG, while ash, sycamore and beech respond well. Fruitwoods are generally more difficult and dry with mixed results, mainly due to their finer texture.

Calculations

PEG is dissolved in water, with the strength of the solution, the temperature and the soaking time all being important. A 30 per cent solution is best, produced by mixing 53oz (1.5kg) of PEG in 3.5 litres (6 pints) of water to make a total volume of 5 litres (8.8 pints). Use a hydrometer to check the density of the solution which should have a specific gravity of about 1.05 at 70°F (21°C). As the wood absorbs PEG, the solution gradually becomes more diluted. Adding more PEG occasionally will restore it to its original strength.

The beauty of PEG seasoning is the lack of specialist equipment it requires. Only a non-metallic container of some sort deep enough to allow the wood to be fully immersed is needed. A plastic dustbin or a central heating header tank is ideal. Insulating it with polystyrene will also help to maintain the soaking temperature. The penetration into the timber is much quicker if the solution is kept warm, ideally around 140°F (60°C). A small pad heater is sufficient to maintain this level and costs very little to run.

The length of time you leave the wood to soak is rather difficult to determine as there are so many variable factors to consider. As a general rule, pieces with a wall thickness of 1–1.5in (25–38mm) usually take three or four weeks at 70°F (21°C) and SG 1.05. By increasing the temperature to 140°F (60°C), the time is reduced dramatically to just one or two weeks.

Most homegrown hardwoods are suitable for treatment. PEG has also been used successfully to treat timbers which are difficult to season conventionally. As it's so hygroscopic, PEG attracts moisture to the surface

▶ **PEG treated timber is much easier to cut.**

which reduces the moisture gradient and also prevents drying cracks which can develop into shakes or even honeycombing. A quick pre-soak in PEG before air or kiln drying virtually eliminates surface checking on thick planks and burrs and prevents the development of initial surface shrinkage or internal compression.

When you're preparing pieces of wood for PEG treatment it's vital that you preserve the original moisture content until they are ready to soak. Another tip is to cut them as near to the final size as possible to maximize the penetration and to minimize the wastage of PEG.

Once your wood has been completely soaked, it needs to be dried thoroughly before finishing. It can be dried naturally in the air or, if you are more adventurous and allowed free reign in the kitchen, a quick warm through in the oven works wonders – although this sometimes darkens the timber and gives a new aroma to the Sunday roast! I've also found that sticking a few pieces in the back of the airing cupboard works well.

Final stages

Once it's pickled, it's important to finish the wood as PEG is hygroscopic and therefore will soon start to pick up moisture from the air making the wood feel damp. The surface will also quickly develop a mildew mould. This can stain quite deeply, so keep a careful look out for this taking place.

A batch of PEG solution will store in the tank, yet it often develops a thick scum of mould on the top. Overcome this with a small dose of the fungicide that is usually supplied with the PEG, if you run out use a garden fungicide. Although keep checking on the SG and add more PEG or water to maintain the concentration.

Treated wood is generally much easier to machine as the PEG lubricates the tool as you cut. Sanding, on the other hand, is problematic as the abrasive clogs quickly. One of the main disadvantages of PEG, referred to previously, is the limitation it imposes on the type of finish you can use. Finishes like shellac, some varnishes and lacquer simply will not take.

The only alternatives are polyurethane, oil or plastic coating. Gluing PEG treated material generates similar problems. Ideally, the surface should be cleaned with methanol before gluing to remove surface traces. PVA and aliphatic glues are less successful, so use an epoxy or resorcinol based material for full strength.

141

Selecting Wood

10

In the UK we're lucky to have a good supply of different species to choose from, homegrown and imported, hardwood and softwood each with their own unique set of characteristics.

Choose carefully

Things become complicated when there is considerable variation in factors such as colour, texture and grain structure, even within the same species. Therefore, simply specifying a species is not necessarily enough to guarantee obtaining timber that looks the way you expect. Consequently, where factors such as figure, grain and colour are critical, it's essential to look carefully at particular timber before purchasing.

Distinguishing factors

Inevitably, each piece of timber is totally unique. Many of these distinguishing factors are obvious even to the layman. Yet we woodworkers also need to understand some of the less obvious features such as density, strength and response to humidity changes. These variables can then be accounted for within the design, to produce a fully functional piece which maximizes the material's potential.

The first decision is whether to use hardwood or softwood. These terms do not refer to the hardness of the timber as you might assume, but are actually a botanical classification based on the timber's anatomical structure. Consequently, some hardwoods may actually be quite soft and vice versa.

▼ The UK has a good supply of both homegrown and imported species.

There is considerable variation even within the same species.

▼ Accounting for working properties within the design maximizes the potential of the timber.

Hardwoods grow in most parts of the world and are usually selected for making fine furniture. Although they're more expensive, they're also more durable with a greater range of colour and figure. Many of the more exotic hardwoods exhibit a dazzling array of colours ranging from creamy white to rich black. They also have an almost continual growth cycle producing some very fine textured timber. However, their annual rings may be difficult to distinguish.

▼ Exotic timbers often exhibit a dazzling array of colours.

Fast grown softwoods are mainly used for construction and basic joinery work.

Softwoods, on the other hand, are generally light in colour with a narrow range from yellow to mid-brown. As they are fast growing, their annual rings are very easy to distinguish, but there is little natural figure apart from areas surrounding defects, such as knots. Being relatively inexpensive, softwoods are mainly used for construction and basic joinery work. Although in some Scandinavian countries there is still a strong demand for pine furniture.

Purchasing timber

In the UK, small quantities of hardwood are sold by the cubic foot. A cubic foot is theoretically a piece 12in x 12in x 12in (305mm x 305mm x 305mm),

totalling 1728in^3. In practice, this then needs to be converted to more realistic dimensions, so a piece 12ft (3.7m) long of 12in x 1in (305mm x 25mm) is still 1ft^3 (0.3m^3), as is a 6ft (1.8m) piece of 8in x 3in (200mm x 75mm).

The calculation is:

$$\frac{\textbf{length x width x thickness}}{\textbf{1728}} = \textbf{cubic foot}$$

So if, for instance, you are quoted £60 per cubic foot for a piece of oak, and you need the price for a piece 8 foot x 9in x 1½in (2.4m x 229mm x 38mm) the cost will be:

$$\frac{\textbf{96 x 9 x 1.5}}{\textbf{1728}} = \textbf{0.75 cubic foot, } \quad \textbf{0.75 x 60 = £45}$$

Waney edged boards are very irregular in shape.

▶ Square edging is a
very wasteful process...

Homegrown timber is often sold as waney edged. The natural bark edge on either side of the planks makes measuring the width slightly more subjective, particularly if the boards are very irregular in shape. Normally, three measurements are taken along the length, including half the wane, with the average taken as the width. However, some merchants only use a single width dimension; measuring the board one third of the length up from the butt end and taking the width from here, including half the wane.

Imported hardwood is nearly always square edged to minimize the amount of wasted shipping space. Yet to maximize the yield, individual planks may be left in random widths and lengths. This square edging process is obviously wasteful. You will also be made to pay a premium price for square edged boards and even more for boards of just one width.

More exotic species, particularly those with lots of internal defects, are usually sold in log form and exported whole. They are then cut by the importer

◀ ...producing vast
amounts of scrap.

Many exotic species contain lots of internal defects.

Very expensive timbers are not usually sold by weight.

and the boards are sold including any defects. These boards may include huge amounts of sapwood, for example padauk, or a lot of central degrade, like ovankol. In extreme cases very expensive timbers, such as snakewood, lignum vitae and cocobolo, may even be sold by weight to take into account their small size and wasteful conversion. Burrs are also sold this way as they're impossible to measure accurately.

Grading

Many of the more usual imported species are graded into one of several categories to account for their natural variation and to ensure uniformity of supply between the different sources. This grading is based on the amount of defect-free wood in a particular board; the greater the amount, the better the grade. The best grades are referred to as firsts or firsts and seconds (FAS). Lesser grades, which have an increasing amount of defects, are called selects and commons. As a guide, there will be around 85 per cent of perfect wood in an FAS grade board, but only 65 per cent in a No.1 common board. Grading is a highly skilled and labour intensive process which requires each board to be examined on both sides, the defects accounted for, then the grade quickly calculated and marked.

Boards are normally graded with any defect accounted for and marked.

▷ Structural timber may be mechanically stress graded.

Softwoods, on the other hand, are virtually always cut to standard square edged dimensions and sold by the foot or metre run. This makes it much easier to calculate an exact cost. As with hardwoods, they're graded for evenness of the grain and the amount of allowable defects, such as knots or bark. Timber for structural work may also be stress graded. The wood is passed through a machine which applies a measured amount of bending, then tests the reaction of each piece, before stamping it with the appropriate grade.

When you are purchasing timber, remember that the dimensions quoted to you are usually rough sawn, so you have to allow for planing all round.

This will reduce the dimensions by at least $\frac{1}{8}$in (3mm) depending on the species. Also, bear in mind that the size may be based on a pre-drying dimension. As some shrinkage inevitably occurs as the wood dries, a 3in (75mm) thick piece for example, may actually become 2¾in (70mm). There is no convention on this, some mills may cut oversize to allow for shrinkage and provide the full thickness, while other mills may not.

Prepared softwood is always based on the original rough sawn size. So for instance, planed all round a piece of timber 3in x 2in (75mm x 50mm) is normally finished at 2¾in x 1⅞in (70mm x 47mm).

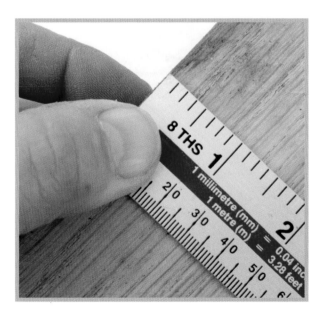

◁ Some saw mills cut oversize to allow for shrinkage during drying.

▽ Prepared softwood is always based on the original rough sawn size.

Selecting and estimating timber

Unfortunately, the whole process of selecting timber is burdened with a huge number of variables, most of which are out of your control. This is just the frustrating nature of timber with all its inherent natural characteristics. Boards are rarely perfect or uniform and often include natural or man-made defects. While there are no definitive rules for selecting timber, there are some guidelines to help with estimations and costing. You will also soon be able to draw upon your own experience.

Unless you have the space and finances to keep huge stocks of timber in a variety of species, you will need to purchase enough material for each individual project. Yet just how much should you buy? Hardwood in particular is relatively expensive, so you don't want to buy more than necessary. Having said this, buying too little can be false economy, as you then waste time returning to buy just a small amount to complete the job. This assumes, of course, that you can get more matching material; in my experience it probably won't match! So the first lesson is to make sure you buy plenty. It's cheaper in the long run and any leftover

pieces can go into your timber store for future use. The first stage in estimating the amount you require is always to take a close look at the cutting list. From this you can calculate the theoretical requirement for each piece in cubic feet.

For the calculations use the formula shown earlier:

$$\frac{\text{Length x width x thickness}}{1728} = \text{volume in cubic feet}$$

Yet although this is a useful starting point, this figure is rather deceptive and in reality it bears little resemblance to what is actually needed.

Potential problems

It's very unusual to find boards that are exactly the right width, unfortunately. Inevitably, some of them will need cutting from wider material. The wider the board, the more waste is generated and this can be significant.

For example, if you require an 8ft (2.4m) board of 7in x 1in (178mm x 25mm) material, you will probably need to buy an 8in x 1in (203mm x 25mm) resulting in a 16 per cent wastage. That's £8 waste at £50 ft³, and you haven't even started yet!

◄ **Home users are rarely able to keep large stocks of timber.**

▷ **Randomly selected boards may be difficult to match.**

The same problems occur with length. Once again the longer the pieces you require, the more wastage there will be. For this reason, you should always start cutting out the widest and longest pieces first, then cut the smaller ones from the waste produced. This will go some way towards minimizing the costs. Bear in mind that the ends of each board may also contain drying splits or checks which only appear as you start cutting. The solution is to cut off full width pieces, although the waste percentage then begins to multiply alarmingly.

▲ **Cutting down wide boards generates significant waste.**

◁ **End splits and checks may be invisible until you start crosscutting.**

▼ **Working around large knots can also increase the waste percentage.**

▷ **Staining from the stickers may be difficult to remove even with heavy planing.**

Even after the boards are cut to the right measurements other problems may suddenly appear, such as extensive sapwood bands down the edges, or large knots in the face. Sometimes the knots are acceptable as in character grade flooring, yet often they affect the appearance or structural quality to such an extent that they must be cut out. The waste then starts to rapidly accumulate along with a skipful of very expensive firewood!

Moisture often has a part to play in this wastage process, mainly during the drying stage. Apart from the normal drying defects, such as checking and distortion, careless placing of the stickers in a stack may cause varying degrees of bowing and warping. The stickers should all be placed directly in line with each other. Using the wrong type of sticker or leaving it protruding too far may cause surface stains. These require some serious planing work to remove with a consequent loss of thickness.

You can exacerbate these problems with careless storage, even with dry timber. Don't just throw it carelessly onto a rack. Unless the boards are stored properly, they will soon cup and twist, seriously reducing the possible yield of flat stock. Timber is precious, so respect it.

▷ **Timber should be stacked carefully to minimize further distortion.**

◁ Cutting shaped components is another wasteful process.

▽ An uneconomical cut is often the best way to get the best grain match.

The components you're cutting may not necessarily be straight either. This can be another source of considerable waste, especially if you require a particular grain orientation for the finished appearance or to maximize strength. If you're matching pieces side by side to make wider sections, there is often a price to pay. You may have to cut quite wastefully so as to get the best grain match, or if the grain is being used as a design element.

If you require thin material, the temptation is to assume that slicing a thicker piece in half will be sufficient. Yet as soon as you start re-sawing, any growing and drying stresses are released and the

boards will often bow quite dramatically along their length. They will then require a lot of planing to restore their flat and parallel surfaces. In my experience, re-sawing boards requires a wastage allowance of at least 50 per cent, so if possible only buy thin material that has already been pre-cut and dried.

Additionally, don't assume that the size of boards will necessarily be the same when they're finished. 1in (25mm) boards for example, unless sawn significantly oversize to allow for shrinkage and any warping and cupping during drying, will finish at $7/8$in (22mm) or less. This is particularly significant if you're machining up longer lengths. Remember that $1/8$in (3mm) of bow across the width will need planing out from both sides resulting in an overall loss of $1/4$in (6mm). So if you need to finish at 1in (25mm), then it's necessary to buy $1\frac{1}{4}$in (32mm). This high wastage factor varies with different species. Some are better than others, but there is probably a 25 per cent allowance needed here.

◁ Re-sawing boards again creates significant waste.

Going from a rough sawn section to planed all round can mean a loss of up to 25 per cent.

Even the best woodworkers make mistakes. So not purchasing enough spare material to replace the odd wrongly cut component can become an issue and increase your costs. You may also need to select particularly well-figured pieces, perhaps for a table top or drawer front. Yet cutting the material to maximize this figure may not necessarily make the most efficient use of your stock. It's always best to buy in a couple of spare boards, particularly if the figure is going to be a major part of the design.

Where to buy timber
Larger sources

Your next decision is where to buy your timber from. If you're looking for softwoods or common hardwood species, such as oak or ash, a local builder's merchant may be able to help. They usually stock whitewood in prepared sizes and redwood in rough sawn planks, so this should cover most of your softwood requirements. However, their hardwood stock is probably limited to a bit of American oak and some anonymous red material euphemistically described as 'mahogany' and usually of Far Eastern origin.

For a better selection, you will need to go to a dedicated timber merchant, some specialize in either homegrown or imported timbers, with the bigger ones doing both. Having said this, many of these places are geared towards trade customers purchasing large quantities of wood. They will may not be particularly receptive to your small order for two boards of maple, especially if you want to rifle through a pile of neatly stacked boards to select the best quarter sawn material. Some of the smaller mills may allow you to do this, but will charge you extra for the privilege. Also, bear in mind that the cubic foot prices quoted are probably based on quantity and a hefty premium may well be applied for smaller quantities.

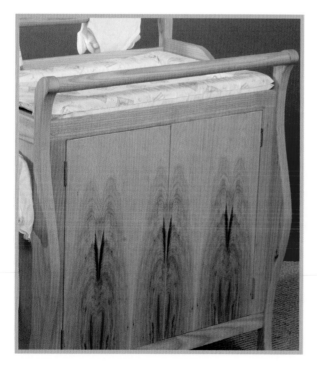

Selecting for figure does not always make the most efficient use of material.

◁ Not all timber
merchants are geared up
to supply small quantities.

▽ Allow at least 75 per
cent on the finished sizes when
buying waney edged material.

Smaller sources

Smaller mills specializing in homegrown material are
usually more accommodating. These are a good place to
spend a pleasant hour or two rummaging among piles
of waney edged timber. Yet here lies another problem,
waney edged boards are difficult to measure and to
estimate for volume. Although there are guidelines
for measurement, it all comes down to one person's
opinion. You will also inevitably end up buying a lot
of waste. When buying natural edged material, I always
allow at least 75 per cent on the finished sizes.

When selecting boards which are evenly matched
for both colour and grain, your best option is to buy
consecutive slices off a log. Some mills will stock timber
in this form, either homegrown hardwood or imported
material. This provides a consistency that's not possible
when buying square edged stock. This latter option is
usually just a random selection of boards from different
trees sorted for size rather than colour or figure.

Smaller homegrown mills only offer rough-sawn
or air-dried timber. The term air-dried needs to be
taken with a pinch of salt, as some unscrupulous sellers
will claim that material is air-dried even if it's only been
cut for a few months. With experience you will soon be
able to judge for yourself how long ago it was cut, both
by the appearance and the weight of the boards. Also,
don't assume that just because the logs have obviously

◁ Consecutive slices
of a log are essential
to match the figure.

▽ Square edged stock is
usually a random selection
of boards.

⚠ **Clean, flat boards split and distort when drying generating yet more waste.**

▶ **Kiln-dried material stored under cover requires initial conditioning in a warm room before use.**

been cut for some years that they're completely dry. I would recommend taking a moisture meter with you to check exactly what you're buying.

Air drying rarely reduces the moisture content to 15 per cent or below, even during a hot summer. So you will need to cost this in and allow time for it to dry out further in a warm room before use. Drying the wood also inevitably results in the appearance of defects. The boards may look deceptively flat and clean at the mill, but as soon as they start to dry cracks and splits may well appear. The boards then take on weird and wonderful shapes, resulting in huge amounts of waste.

The ideal is to buy kiln-dried material, usually only available from the bigger mills. More often than not this is square edged material that has been stacked in a drying chamber and the moisture removed under controlled conditions to about 10 per cent.

Bear in mind that after kiln drying the material is usually stacked back outside under cover. It's therefore likely to reabsorb moisture to around the 12 to 14 per cent mark. So, even this wood will require some initial conditioning in a warm room before use.

▶ **Shorts are a cheaper way of buying otherwise good quality hardwood.**

Saving money

Quite often, small woodworking projects only require short pieces of timber, so it might be worth asking your timber merchant if they have any 'shorts'. As the name suggests, these are offcuts of longer boards, normally 3–6ft (0.91–1.82m) in length. They're also often of FAS quality, although technically such short pieces are not allowed under FAS grading rules. In my experience they're usually very good quality, much easier to handle and considerably cheaper than full length stock which will probably be cut shorter anyway.

Another good source is 'kiln samples', although these need to be treated with care. These are even smaller boards, usually around 3ft (0.9m) long, which are placed strategically around the inside of a kiln as test pieces during the drying process. They may be rather variable with regards to moisture content, but if you're aware of the potential pitfalls these samples can be very good value for money.

In your quest for cheap timber, don't forget less obvious sources. Traditional old furniture, as opposed to antique, has very little value these days and is frequently just dumped or burnt. This is a shame as much of it contains very usable material often of a

quality unobtainable today. So keep your eyes open, especially as it's usually free for the taking. Just watch out for nails and screws!

It might also be worth tracking down one of the new timber recycling depots. These stock a wide range of previously used timber in all shapes and sizes, either for re-use as it is, or for converting into other dimensions. Although superficially messy, much of this timber is often of a far higher quality than newer material. It has also been stored well, so you can be confident that the moisture content is low enough for immediate use.

◀ **Home conversion is difficult, although possible for small or special logs.**

◀ **Always replace boards neatly when selecting from a stack.**

▼ **The figure will change from crown to quarter to cut as you move towards the centre.**

It's also quite feasible to convert your own logs for small scale jobs using a wide blade on the bandsaw and a suitable jig to safely guide the log. Yet, attempting to season logs in the round is rarely successful as they inevitably split. Slicing them into boards creates some usable material as well as lots of waste, so this is really only a serious option for special logs.

Pick your boards

If a mill agrees to you rummaging around and picking your own boards, the selection process becomes part of the whole making experience. The more care you put in at this stage the better the end result will be, particularly if you're making fine pieces of furniture.

It's hard work turning over a pile of boards, especially if they're thick. Yet try to look at each and every one before making your selection, if possible. Bear in mind that it takes a great deal of time to form the carefully piled stacks, so always put them back neatly after you have made your selection.

Start by pulling out all the obvious straight and flat boards, initially two or three times the quantity that's needed. The twisted ones might be usable when cut into short pieces, but you don't want to handicap yourself at this early stage, so only select the best. Check the edges for sapwood, as this affects the colour and may be a haven for woodworm. If this is a concern return them to the stack.

Next, look at the figure and grain characteristics, check that these are similar in all the boards. If you're sorting through a consecutive stack from a round log the figure will change from crown to quarter as you move towards the centre of the stack, so select relevant boards for particular jobs. If the stack is made up of random boards the figure may vary dramatically as there will be pieces from several different trees. Again select only those that match closely to avoid them looking totally different when planed up and polished. Any pieces with bad knots need to be judged carefully. If the rest of the board is well figured then they are often quite usable provided you can work between the knots. If they're likely to restrict your cutting choices later, put the board back. Also check that an allowance has been made for the knot in the price.

◀ Large knots may restrict your cutting options, so avoid these if possible.

By now you've probably cut your initial selection by around half. Your final choice should be based on colour. This may vary greatly from board to board as pieces from different trees are all mixed together. Older boards in particular may well have become discoloured with age, therefore you may find it difficult to judge their true colour. Although shaving a small patch with a hand plane or chisel will usually reveal any treasures which lie beneath.

Best guess!

Estimating and accurately pricing timber is a job fraught with difficulty. Only experience will show you how to accurately predict the likely wastage, depending on the sizes and the species involved. As a general rule, take the actual requirement from the cutting list and double it as a starting point for pricing. This is the minimum price which can be increased if either the particular species or the sizes are awkward.

▶ A light shaving will quickly reveal what lies beneath the weathered surface.

Reclaimed Timber

Good quality timber is such an expensive and precious resource these days that it should always be used sparingly. Recycling old timber which would otherwise be consigned to the bonfire is even better. There is something immensely satisfying about rescuing cracked and dirty pieces of wood, then giving them a new lease of life.

One man's waste is another man's treasure

An estimated 3000 tons of potentially reusable timber is scrapped everyday in the UK, most of this is burnt or ends up as landfill. Obviously it's important to differentiate between timber which is suitable for reuse and timber which is not. Although sometimes the boundary between the two is distinctly blurred.

Reusing timber is not just a means of saving money, more importantly it's about maximizing raw materials. While timber is a relatively quick renewable resource, this isn't an excuse for simply tossing yet another piece of 'scrap' onto the wood burner. What's more, unlike with a lot of other supposedly recyclable materials, there is very little energy input involved in the recycling process.

Definitions

Before we go any further, it's important to distinguish between 'recycling' and 'reclaiming'. I would suggest that recycling applies to reusing timber or timber products in the way in which they were originally used. The best examples of this are old beams or floorboards and finished items like doors, windows and skirting boards. These are reused just as they were when taken out of their original site, often requiring only minimum cleaning or repair. There are now dozens of yards all

▼ Reclaimed beams.

◀ Old beams may be on
their second or third use.

over the country specializing in 'architectural salvage'. These yards stock vast amounts of material ready to be incorporated into new buildings, some of which may already be on its second or third cycle. Oak beams previously used as ships timbers are a classic example. Reclaiming, on the other hand, implies that the original timber is extracted from its current form, then cut up and reused in a completely different form. Old beams are often re-sawn into thin planks for use in furniture making, while floorboards and antique furniture are equally good sources of 'new' raw material. Fortunately, more and more people are becoming

▶ Old furniture is a good
source of quality material.

aware of the potential for reclaiming timber resulting in several new specialized businesses which buy and sell timber for reuse emerging. Education authorities and local councils are just some of the organizations enhancing their green credentials by donating material for reuse. In addition to the environmental and economic benefits, reclaiming timber often provides access to wood of unrivalled quality and size and to species that are no longer commercially or sometimes legally available. The tightening of export regulations concerning many of the previously freely available hardwood species has made an increasing number difficult to source. Reusing old timber overcomes these problems, though admittedly supply is relatively small and inconsistent.

Sources

A little lateral thinking can open up dozens of potential and varied sources of inexpensive or even free material. Some of these are likely to be one-offs, relying on you being in the right place at the right time, but others may be more consistent.

Here are a few examples of reclaimed material sources I've used. You will find many more just by keeping your eyes open!

Waste material

Pallets are often suggested as a source of raw material, yet their scope is rather limited for anything other than utilitarian projects. Standard ones are usually made from very poor quality softwood and even the thicker

▼ **Specialized reclaiming businesses are now beginning to appear.**

▶ Standard pallets contain very little usable material.

▼ Custom made pallets may contain more interesting timbers...

▲ ...and you can usually salvage some very usable stock.

corner blocks often contain too many nail holes to be of any use. However, look out for custom-made pallets as these often contain quite chunky sections of interesting timbers, native to the country of export.

I regularly visit a local factory which imports machine spares from America and uses specially made pallets containing a mixture of timbers. My most recent acquisition from here contained a mixture of robinia, basswood and oak, and was completely free. I admit that much of it was of very poor quality with lots of heart shakes, deep splits and major nail holes, yet I

was still able to cut out a useful selection of interesting looking pieces. Packing cases are another good source. I once found one made from Brazilian tulipwood! Admittedly the timber was very thin, contained lots of sapwood and was quite badly checked, but there was still some very usable material for box making.

The beauty of using 'waste' material is that people are more than glad to get rid of it, particularly with the current regulations regarding waste disposal. Suppliers are often very pleased to see otherwise scrap material being used fruitfully. I was given the opportunity to poke around a local barn just before it was demolished. The structure had been supported by a variety of timber uprights from which I was able to chainsaw off a few likely looking lengths. Although much of this was softwood, some additional supports had been added

▶ **The author found this old barn undergoing demolition.**

later which amazingly turned out to be purpleheart, containing only a few bolt holes. I can't tell you why this species was used, but I was very grateful. At the back of the barn I also found a collection of old beds, many of which were just veneered onto softwood. However, one contained some useful looking timber in an indeterminate hardwood, probably walnut; all will be revealed when it goes through the planer.

Unwanted items

Don't overlook the value of old furniture. Sale rooms are frequently overstocked with items which are relatively worthless to the owner and which they're often glad to give away to clear the space. Through careful selection you can often find a lot of usable material, although check carefully for woodworm. Occasionally, you may come across gems like these carved panels from an old wardrobe door shown below right. With a good clean, stain and polish they will look spectacular in their second phase of life. Old worktops and wardrobe sides in particular contain significant amounts of 'clean' timber, with very little

▶ **Some of the wood was highly exotic timber.**

▶ These old bed ends
turned out to be solid walnut.

▼ Check old material
carefully for worm infestation.

in the way of nail or screw holes. This tatty looking panelling in the picture below turned out to be genuine Brazilian mahogany. In addition, watch out for old established shops being refitted. These have usually been furnished with properly made counters, not like the modern chipboard and glass jobs. Breaking these

◀ Old carved panels just
need a clean and polish.

▼ Reclaimed panelling
in Brazilian mahogany.

◀ **Old shop fittings in beautiful yellow pine.**

▶ **Even woodturners can use thin material by laminating them into something bigger...**

▼ **... then gluing them together.**

up will yield a good harvest of wide and thoroughly dry panels, which are virtually unobtainable today. Also be on the look out for any old hardware. Even very thin material can be laminated to create something larger. Thin boards can be used to make deep bowl blanks by cutting out a series of rings at an angle before gluing them together as a stack. Alternatively, slice the thin material into longitudinal staves then glue them together to form deep hollow blanks.

▷ Ornaments found in
charity shops are a good
source of more exotic timbers.

▽ Old bowling woods often
contain solid *Lignum vitae*.

Try looking around your local charity shop for existing
pieces of woodwork that can be reworked. The heavy
and clumsy candlesticks above were purchased with
just small change, yet subsequent reworking showed
them to be a species of valuable *Lignum vitae*. Many
species like this are now CITES listed and cannot be
purchased legally, but there is no problem in recycling
existing material. You may also find more lignum in
the form of old bowling woods. For the ornamental
turners, genuine ivory can still be fund in old billiard
balls and excellent quality ebony is often found as
ornaments. Again these can be cut up and reworked.

Unexpected finds

My eye was recently caught by the tip in our local
builder's yard in which some old railway sleepers
were poking out from some nettles. Many of these are
heavily impregnated softwood, full of grit and totally
unsuitable. Yet occasionally you can be lucky enough
to come across some hardwood ones. These particular
ones turned out to be jarrah, which is very difficult to
cut but certainly worth the effort. These were free for
the taking, although it was a struggle.

◁ Old hardwood railway sleepers are also
a good source of heavy section material.

◄ The surface coating of the sleeper disguises the beautiful timber within.

▼ Old telegraph poles are inevitably softwood and of little use.

Gateposts can also be a rich source of reclaimed material, especially useful in big sections for turning and carving. However, be wary of using those made from old telegraph poles. These are heavily impregnated with preservatives and only contain a small core of usable timber, virtually always incorporating the heart of the tree. More importantly, old material like this was often treated in the days before health and safety became an issue. The preservatives they contain are a deadly cocktail of arsenic and chromium compounds that can be released when you start cutting into them.

▼ They also contain the heart of the tree which is liberally soaked in potentially harmful preservatives.

◁ Old gate posts may also contain a variety of metal work.

▽ Yew gate posts contain a sound hardwood core...

▶ ... which is quickly converted into usable pieces on the bandsaw.

Old gateposts may also contain a variety of metal work, which surprisingly is sometimes an advantage provided it's visible. Obviously you need to cut well clear of it, but the metal frequently produces some fantastic colouration in timbers such as oak, chestnut and yew. Those made from branch wood are most useful. In our local area there's a tradition of creating gateposts using yew roundwood. The sapwood rots away quickly and the post is then discarded. Yet cutting through it reveals a remaining core of sound hardwood, although once again this will contain the central pith. A few minutes work on the bandsaw to remove the worst of the rotted material produces some very usable large section yew blanks that would have cost a fortune to purchase.

▶ **Even apparently rotting material may be better than you think.**

▼ **Once again the crosscut reveals usable timber within.**

▲ **Deep cracks can be incorporated into more rustic designs.**

▼ **Old piles from piers and sea defences were always made from durable timbers like greenheart and elm.**

Never overlook anything, even the most unlikely pile of old wood may unearth something useful. In this case, a heap of seemingly well-rotted posts actually contained some very nicely coloured English oak. Depending on your taste, you can either cut away all the serious cracking or incorporate it into a more rustic design. Another very interesting source of reclaimed material is the piles used as part of piers, sea defences and lock gates. These are always made from highly durable timbers, like greenheart and elm, to cope with being continually submerged.

▶ Newel posts and table legs from reclamation yards can often be reworked.

▼ Check the moisture content, as the timber may still be wet.

Industrial sources

Reclamation yards will often stock heavy section turnings in the form of newel posts or table legs that can be reworked into more useful projects. Yet just because this material is old, it's not necessarily dry. In fact some of it may still be very wet, so check the moisture content with a meter before you start working it to save any disappointment. Although it's not strictly reclaimed timber, local joinery firms use a range of the

▼ The skip at a local factory may produce usuable timber.

▶ **Even the author's minute pieces of waste are taken by a local pen maker.**

more commercial hardwood species. Wood that they regard as useless offcuts is probably still very usable, so it's always worth hunting through the skip. Once again they're often glad to get rid of it. Everything has a use, no matter how small. I'm regularly visited by a pen maker who finds my minimal 'scrap' a rich source of raw material for his projects.

Personal project

I have had a little console table project in mind for some time, I'm just waiting for the right material. So when I recently spotted a pile of old garden furniture piled up in a bonfire ready for a match, it seemed too good an opportunity to miss. After a polite request the wood was mine for the taking.

Back in the workshop and after spending a few minutes with a big hammer, I soon had the makings of some very usable timber which I suspected to be iroko. Although the outside was still dirty and checked, the underlying timber appeared to be perfectly sound. I soon cut out enough usable pieces for use in my project. A great example of putting 'waste' to good use.

Take note

The only downside with second-hand timber, particularly when it's been used outside, is that it's often impregnated with grit, so give it all a good brush before you start. A quick pass over the planer often reveals some wonderful grain beneath and fortunately much of the surface cracking is usually only very shallow. There may also be screws or nails which must be removed before you start. You only have to catch

◀ **This old garden furniture was rescued from a bonfire …**

▶ ... a few minutes with a large hammer, produced some very usable pieces.

▼ Skim over with the planer to remove the weathered finish.

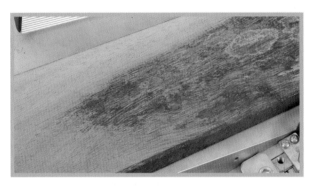

▲ Beware of the embedded nails and screws as they will damage cutting blades.

one nail on the saw or planer for the blades to need regrounding. What was initially very cheap timber then becomes expensive.

The reward is in turning what was dirty and abandoned material destined for the fire into a piece of furniture that will hopefully last forever, or at least until someone fancies reworking it into something completely different.

Hopefully this brief foray into the world of wood recycling has stirred you into re-thinking your timber supply chain. It's obviously not a total solution, particularly for large scale projects, but I regularly manage to restock my shelves with some very nice examples of rare and expensive species without even reaching for my wallet!

◀ From bonfire to finished table.

Health and Safety

12

Wood is perceived to be the ultimate natural material and therefore is usually not associated with any health risks. Unfortunately, working with wood can occasionally be detrimental to our health.

Recognizing risks

In the past, safety in the workshop centred on the potential dangers of machinery and tools. However, the emphasis has recently switched to the less obvious hazards of dust. This is becoming increasingly recognized as a serious threat to health, especially as the effects are cumulative with serious symptoms only emerging once it's too late. Fortunately, we've now become aware of the potential dangers of long-term exposure to dust. It's very important that we recognize it as a real risk and take positive steps to minimize it.

Many books, even those published relatively recently, neglect to mention the potential hazards of using toxic timbers. Yet long-term exposure to wood dust from sanding, sawing or planing can lead to many serious medical conditions, including asthma, rhinitis, conjunctivitis, even cancer of the respiratory tract and dermatitis. Many of the symptoms only appear after a lifetime of working with wood and usually only after working with a particularly toxic species.

However, it's also possible to overstate these dangers, especially as people have been working safely with wood for hundreds of years. It's only with recent advances in medical testing and research that concerns have begun to grow, almost to the opposite extreme. Although many of the findings are not entirely consistent, it's better to be aware of the potential risks, so you can take appropriate precautions.

▶ Long-term exposure to dust is a real threat that must be minimized.

Respiratory dangers
Dust

The main concern with dust is that it's an insidious problem. Initial exposure rarely causes any immediate issues. It's only when symptoms start to develop that we take any notice, by then it's usually too late. Our respiratory systems are actually well-adapted to coping with most of the dust. Additionally, the bulk of the waste is usually fairly heavy shavings, often classed as 'nuisance dust', with particles larger than five microns in size becoming trapped and expelled by the mucous membranes in your lungs. While these cause discomfort, there's no lasting damage, although prolonged exposure may result in long-term health problems. It's only when you start operations such as sanding that the much finer dust is produced with almost invisibly sized particles.

◀ Hardwood dust is considered more hazardous than softwood.

▼ Many woodturners overcome dust allergies by only working wet wood.

While I'm not sufficiently qualified to give a scientific opinion, it's my understanding that it's the size of these dust particles that's key. This very fine 'respirable dust' consists of particles below five microns in size which accumulate in the lungs and are not expelled by the body's normal defence mechanism. Continued exposure can lead to serious problems. With all these respiratory dangers, as with many other medical conditions, some people tend to be far more susceptible than others.

Often it's the exotic timbers, such as rosewood and yew, that are assumed to be the only hazardous ones. Yet many of these timbers can cause allergic reactions or skin complaints. Dust from any timber is equally dangerous. In fact species such as ash and beech, particularly when spalted, are well-recognized carcinogens.

Hardwoods are considered to be most harmful, mainly because the softwood particles created by cutting operations are often larger and more fibrous, therefore less able to become airborne. Nevertheless,

fine sanding softwoods often produces hazardous sized particles, so they need to be treated with equal care. Although working green timber produces particles with a high moisture content, these are heavier and consequently less likely to become airborne. For this very reason, several woodturners with respiratory problems have been able to continue working with wood simply by working green timber.

Additional dangers

There are also less obvious dangers to be aware of when cutting wood. For instance, the heat generated when working with some species of timber can release toxic fumes. Terpine fumes, for example, are produced by several species and can lead to chronic lung impairment.

Bio hazards are another cause for concern, with exposure to the micro organisms growing on the wood potentially damaging health. Toxins present in bacteria, moulds and allergenic fungi are thought to cause a wide range of respiratory illnesses.

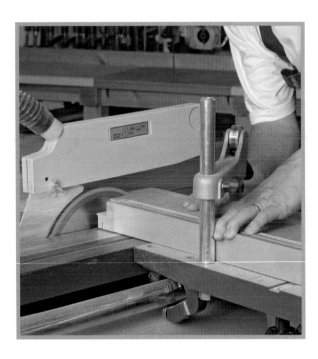

◀ Toxic fumes can
be generated when
cutting certain species

▼ Fungal spores released
when cutting spalted
timbers can cause
respiratory illnesses.

Several of the well-known timber preservative treatments contain a cocktail of copper, chrome and arsenic salts dissolved in water, although these are gradually being replaced by ones which are more user-friendly. While the main danger is to workers who handle the actual liquid preservative, wood dust generated by cutting treated material can be equally toxic. Such material should not be burned either, particularly on barbecues.

Man-made materials are just as likely to cause problems. MDF has long been known to be a potential danger due to the resins involved in its manufacture. These resins, along with impregnated fine dust, are released when the material is machined. They can produce both respiratory and dermatitis type reactions.

Another potential source of irritants comes from materials like dymandwood. This is essentially a plywood made from layers of coloured veneer mixed with resins then baked at a high temperature and pressure to produce a highly decorative material. It's the colourful dyes that are potentially hazardous. So, as with MDF, care should be taken when working this material in order to minimize the risks.

Skin allergies

Probably more obvious than respiratory effects is the problem of skin allergies resulting from handling wood or being exposed to its dust. Between two and five per cent of the population could develop an allergic sensitivity to one of the many compounds found in wood. By far the majority of these toxic compounds are caused by the extractives found in the heartwood of hardwood species.

Contact dermatitis is a result of skin contamination when handling wood and its associated dust during the machining process. Handling it in the form of solid

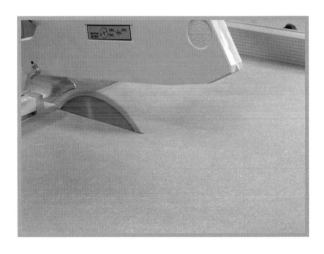

▶ Resins in MDF are potentially harmful.

wood is less likely to cause problems, although some people are so sensitive that they cannot even wear wooden jewellery without a reaction.

The main effect is irritation leading to local inflammation of the skin. This is particularly evident on the hands, arms, face and neck. It's also prominent in areas that get sweaty, which is why it's more common during the summer. The symptoms will remain while there is contact with the source of the irritation, but will generally subside relatively quickly once contact has been removed.

A more debilitating condition is known as sensitisation dermatitis. This can occur with specific timbers, although different people react to different species. In this case, there is no obvious initial problem in using a particular timber. Instead, the person builds up a sensitivity to it, often over a period of years. At some point sensitisation is such that any further minute exposure is enough to cause a severe allergic skin reaction. This allergy is non-reversible and the only solution is not to handle that material again. A further problem is that having become sensitized, other previously safe woods may now produce the same effects, even dust from non-wood sources.

The main cause of these allergies is a group of naturally occurring chemicals called quinines which the tree produces to defend itself against fungal and bacterial attacks. Although they are present in a lot of hardwoods, there are certain species of timber which are notorious for causing severe reactions, some of which can be positively dangerous. These include many of the rosewoods (*Dalbergia spp*), afrormosia (*Pericopsis elata*), greenheart (*Chlorocardium rodiei*), cedar (*Thuja spp*) and yew (*Taxus baccata*). There are many more, refer to the comprehensive list at the end of the chapter.

Other wood dust hazards

The other main potential hazard of dust in the workshop is fire. Accumulations of shavings and dust are a potential problem in themselves, yet the real danger comes from the mix of fine dust and air that pervades the workshop after activities like sanding. A concentration of about 3.5oz (100g) of dust per cubic metre of air is sufficient to form an explosive mixture. This fine dust settles on any flat surface and even clings to the walls. Lifting a tin off a high shelf usually means being deluged with an avalanche of powder-like dust and potentially inhaling a month's supply in one dose!

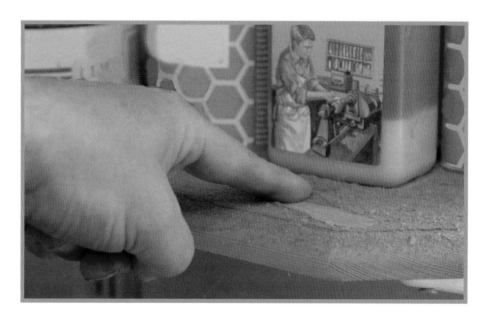

▶ Fine dust soon builds up on the workshop shelves.

◀ Extractors with a coarse filter bag are actually chip collectors.

▼ A fine filter cartridge to replace the cloth bag minimizes the problem of escaping fine dust.

Managing exposure to dust

The control and management of dust is therefore of paramount importance, even in the home workshop. There are several different safety strategies that can be adopted, either singly or in combination, in order to minimize the hazards. Mostly, it's simply common sense. There's also no substitute for good housekeeping and regular cleaning.

Proper dust collection systems installed at the source of the dust are the first line of defence, but these must be suited to the type of dust involved. For real 'belt and braces' protection, install an additional air cleaner to minimize the airborne haze of fine dust. This can be backed up with some form of personal protection, such as a dust mask or air fed helmet. Barrier creams also provide some protection against dermatitis problems. As a last resort, just don't work timbers that are at all doubtful.

Dust extractors

Their main aim is to capture the dust at the source using an extractor of some sort. Although be aware that the standard bag type, low-pressure devices are in fact simply chip collectors. While they appear to suck all the waste away very efficiently, they rely on shifting vast volumes of air, which is then blown back into the atmosphere after having been filtered through the top cloth bag. Unfortunately, these bags can only filter down to about 25 micron sized particles, anything less than that simply passes straight through. Since it's these smaller particles that cause the damage, they're obviously useless as dust collectors. The impression created is one of a cleaner environment, when in fact you are more likely to have concentrated the risk.

If a bag extractor is your only choice, replace the top cloth filter with a fine filter cartridge, as shown in the picture above. Although these are expensive, they effectively retain a lot of the finer dust, apparently down

▼ High pressure
extractors generate less
airflow, but contain the
dust within a sealed canister.

▶ Other high pressure
extractors use a plastic
sack for the waste.

to single micron sized particles. Alternatively, site
the extractor unit outside the workshop, bringing the
pipe in from outside. Unfortunately, this also extracts
your carefully heated workshop air.

High-pressure vacuum extractors have a much
more efficient filtration system and either a sealed
container or a plastic sack to collect the dust. These
will filter the very smallest dust particles, usually
down to a fraction of a micron, as they have several
layers of filtration, combining both paper and cloth
filters. Their only drawback is that they don't move
the same volumes of air as the traditional extractors;
they work on high pressure rather than high volume.
Consequently, the collection spout has to be really
close to the work to be effective.

If you are short of workshop space, there are some
vacuum extractors that can be mounted on the wall
or even under the bench. The solution I've been using
very successfully for several years now is a small vacuum

▶ Several layers of filtration ensure maximum dust collection.

▼ A large spring clip on the end of the pipe means it can be attached to the lathe bed.

▶ The author keeps a small vacuum extractor close to his lathe.

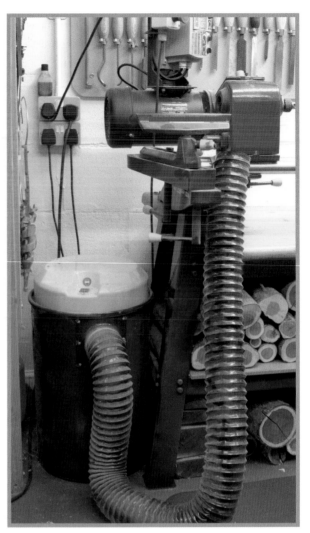

◀ It works equally well for faceplate and spindle turning.

extractor placed within easy reach of the lathe. When I'm just turning, this is coupled to a length of flexible hose with a large spring clip on the end, as well as a short length of rigid pipe which slides in and out of the flexi. The hose is parked on the end of the lathe bed, but as soon as I start sanding it can be relocated at the source of the dust within seconds. The spring clip grips either the lathe bed or any handy bit of casting. The rigid pipe can be slid in or out to ensure that the end is as close as possible to the dust source, either between centres or on faceplate work. Notice the slightly mouthed shaped cut on the end of the pipe to provide even better access.

Protecting yourself

However good your extraction system is, this is not the complete answer. You cannot expect 100 per cent efficiency when attempting to extract at the source. The movement of the abrasive paper coupled with the fan effect of the workpiece means that dust is always diverted away from the extractor nozzle. To protect yourself completely you need to wear a dust mask. The simple disposable cloth or paper ones tend to be inefficient and soon become uncomfortable. Negative pressure rubber respirators are a much better option as they create a better seal and have more sophisticated filters. They don't steam up your glasses either!

▼ Rubber respirators create
a better seal on your face than
cheap cloth dust masks.

▶ Air fed helmets provide
the best level of protection.

For the best protection you cannot beat the air fed helmets which supply you with a stream of clean filtered air, although they are a bit cumbersome to wear.

Although beneficial, these measures only protect you. They don't have any effect on general air quality. Also, what is missed by your extractor is left to settle on any horizontal surface. The ultimate answer for this airborne hazard is an air filter which sucks in the ambient air, cleans it via a filter and then blows it back out into the workshop. I have mine mounted high up in my workshop and it is amazingly efficient, provided I remember to clean the filters occasionally.

In combination, these strategies provide the maximum respiratory protection from dust possible without being particularly intrusive. People with skin allergies may still experience dust related problems, though usually this only occurs with specific timbers. With a small amount of experimentation you can identify your specific triggering allergen. Once you've isolated it and discontinued its use, your skin problems often disappear quite quickly. A good quality barrier cream and surgical gloves may also help.

So whether you are a professional woodworker or simply enjoy the hobby, you can control and minimize the risks. By taking a range of simple precautions you can more or less guarantee your safety without spoiling your enjoyment of working with wood.

◀ An ambient air filter suspended in the
roof of the workshop traps any stray dust.

179

Timbers and their toxicity

This list is by no means exhaustive. I compiled it using many different sources, some of which tend to be a little inconsistent. Yet it covers the symptoms usually associated with the most common woods.

Bear in mind that effects vary in different people and even with different pieces of the same species. The effects are often determined by the growing conditions of the tree.

Timber	Possible effects	Toxic parts
Abura		
Mitragyna stipulosa	Nausea, eye irritation, dizziness	Dust
Afara		
Terminalia superba	Inflammation from splinters	Dust
African blackwood		
Dalbergia melanoylon	Dermatitis, conjunctivitis, sneezing, asthma	Dust
African mahogany		
Khaya ivorensis	Dermatitis, swollen eyelids, nasal cancer	Dust
African walnut		
Lovoa trichilioides	Irritation to mucous membranes, nasal cancer	Dust
Afrormosia		
Pericopsis elata	Dermatitis, rhinitis, asthma, septic splinters	Dust, splinters
Agba		
Gossweilerodendron balsamiferum	Dermatitis	Dust
Alder		
Alnus spp.	Dermatitis, rhinitis, bronchial problems	Dust
Amboyna		
Pterocarpus indicus	Dermatitis, nausea, asthma	Dust

Timber	Possible effects	Toxic parts
American walnut		
Juglans nigra	Irritation to eyes and skin	Dust, wood
Ash		
Fraxinus excelsior	Rhinitis, asthma, decrease in lung function	Dust
Birch		
Betula spp.	Dermatitis, respiratory problems	Dust, wood
Boxwood		
Buxus sempervirens	Dermatitis, irritation to nose, throat and eyes	Dust, wood
Bubinga		
Guibourtia demeusei	Dermatitis, possible skin lesions	Dust
Cedar of Lebanon		
Cedrus libani	Asthma, rhinitis, chest tightness, coughing	Dust
Cherry		
Prunus avium	Breathing difficulties, giddiness	Dust
Chestnut		
Castanea sativa	Dermatitis	Bark, lichens
Cocuswood		
Brya ebenus	Dermatitis	Dust, wood
Cocobolo		
Dalbergia retusa	Dermatitis, conjunctivitis, bronchial asthma	Dust, wood

Timber	Possible effects	Toxic parts
Douglas fir		
Pseudotsuga menziesii	Dermatitis, nasal cancer, irritation to eyes and throat	Dust, wood
Ebony		
Diosyros spp.	Skin inflammation, acute dermatitis, conjunctivitis and sneezing	Dust, wood
European beech		
Fagus sylvatica	Nasal cancer, dermatitis, eye irritation	Dust, leaves, bark
Elm		
Ulmus procera	Dermatitis, irritation of mucous membranes, nasal cancer	Dust
Goncalo alves		
Astronium fraxinifolium	Sensitiser, dermatitis, irritation to skin and eyes	Dust, wood
Greenheart		
Chlorocardium rodiaei	Headache, shortness of breath, disturbed vision, septic splinters	Dust, wood
Guarea		
Guarea spp.	Dermatitis, asthma, nausea, headache and disturbance of vision	Dust, extractives
Hemlock		
Tsuga heterophylla	Dermatitis, rhinitis, eczema, bronchial problems, possible nasal cancer	Dust
Idigbo		
Terminalia ivorensis	Skin and respiratory problems, irritant	Dust

Timber	Possible effects	Toxic parts
Imbuya		
Phoebe porosa	Irritant to eyes, skin and nose	Dust
Indian laurel		
Terminalia alata	Irritant	Dust
Indian rosewood		
Dalbergia spp.	Dermatitis, irritant to eyes, skin and respiratory system	Dust
Ipe		
Tabebuia serratifolia	Dermatitis, shortness of breath, headache, disturbed vision	Dust
Iroko		
Milicia excelsa	Dermatitis, swelling of eyelids, respiratory problems, giddiness	Dust
Jarrah		
Eucalyptus marginata	Irritation to nose, throat and eyes	Dust
Jelutong		
Dyera costulata	Contact allergy	Dust, wood
Keruing		
Dipterocarpus spp.	Dermatitis	Dust
Kingwood		
Dalbergia cearensis	Eye and skin irritant	Dust
Laburnum		
Laburnum anagyroides	Highly toxic	Seeds
Larch		
Larix decidua	Dermatitis, skin rash, respiratory irritation	Dust, bark
Lignum vitae		
Guaiacum officinale	Dermatitis	Dust

Timber	Possible effects	Toxic parts
Makore		
Tieghemella heckelii	Dermatitis, nose and throat irritation, nosebleeds, nausea, can affect blood and central nervous system	Dust, wood
Mansonia		
Mansonia altissima	Dermatitis, nausea, vomiting, nose bleeds, sneezing and asthma	Dust, wood, bark
Maple		
Acer campestre	Sensitizer, reduction in lung function	Dust
Meranti		
Shorea spp.	Dermatitis, irritation to nose, throat and eyes, sinus problems	Dust, wood
Muhuhu		
Brachylaena hutchinsii	Dermatitis	Dust
Mulga		
Acacia aneura	Irritation to mucous membranes and skin, headache, vomiting	Dust
Muninga		
Pterocarpus angolensis	Bronchitis, asthma, dermatitis	Dust
Oak		
Quercus robur	Nasal cancer, dermatitis, sneezing	Dust
Obeche		
Triplochiton scleroxylon	Asthma, sneezing, lung congestion	Dust, wood

Timber	Possible effects	Toxic parts
Olive		
Olea europaea	Respiratory problems, irritant to eyes and skin	Dust
Opepe		
Nauclea diderrichii	Visual disturbance, nosebleeds, dermatitis	Dust, wood
Padauk		
Pterocarpus spp.	Asthma, dermatitis, or vomiting and eyelid swelling	Dust, wood
Pau amarello		
Euxylophora paraensis	Dermatitis	Dust
Pine		
Pinus spp.	Itchy skin, slight fever	Dust, wood
Pink ivory		
Berchemia zeyheri	Dermatitis	Bark, sap
Purpleheart		
Peltogyne pubescens	Irritation to nose, nausea	Dust, wood
Poplar		
Populus spp.	Asthma, dermatitis, bronchitis	Dust, wood
Ramin		
Gonystylus macrophyllum	Skin irritation and infection, cough, sweating and tightness of chest	Dust, wood
Robinia		
Robinia pseudoacacia	Irritation to skin and eyes, nausea	Dust
Rosewood		
Dalbergas spp.	Irritation, dermatitis, respiratory problems	Dust, wood

Timber	Possible effects	Toxic parts
Sapele		
Entandophragma cylindricum	Skin irritation, sneezing	Dust
Satine		
Brosimum spp.	Excessive salivation, nausea, thirst	Dust
Satinwood		
Zanthoxylum flavum	Dermatitis, dizziness, nausea, lethargy, visual disturbance	Dust
Sequoia		
Sequoia sempervirens	Asthma, dermatitis, nasal cancer, pneumonia, respiratory irritant	Dust
Snakewood		
Brosimum guianense	Thirst, salivation, respiratory irritation, nausea	Dust, wood
Spruce		
Picea abies	Irritation to nose and throat	Dust, wood
Tambootie		
Spirostachys africana	Irritation to skin and eyes, listlessness, possible blindness	Dust, bark, sap
Teak		
Tectona grandis	Dermatitis, conjunctivitis, sensitivity to light, irritation to throat and nose, nausea	Dust

Timber	Possible effects	Toxic parts
Thuya burr		
Tetraclinis articulata	Skin irritation	Dust
Tuliptree		
Liriodendron tulipifera	Dermatitis, allergic reactions	Dust
Utile		
Entendophragma utile	Skin irritation	Dust, wood
Walnut		
Juglans regia	Irritation to eyes and skin	Dust
Wenge		
Millettia laurentii	Septic splinters, dermatitis, irritation to eyes and skin, visual disturbance	Dust, wood
Western red cedar		
Thuja plicata	Skin, nasal and throat irritation, dermatitis, rhinitis, asthma, disturbance to central nervous system	Dust, wood, leaves, bark
Willow		
Salix alba	Allergic reaction (similar to aspirin)	Dust
Yew		
Taxus baccata	Dermatitis, headache, congestion of lungs, nausea, visual disturbance	Dust, wood, leaves
Zebrano		
Microberlinia brazzavillensis	Sensitizer, irritation to eyes and skin	Dust, wood

Glossary

Angiosperm The class of plants with their seeds enclosed in a cover of some sort, such as a cone or fruit.

Air-dried Timber that has reached its equilibrium moisture content with the outdoor environment.

Anisotropic Not having the same physical properties in all directions.

Annual ring The layer of wood a tree gains in a single year, made up of a band of earlywood and a band of latewood.

Bandsaw mill A large portable bandsaw that is towed to a felling location for converting butts on site.

Bark The protective outer layer of the tree's trunk, including the inner living bark and the outer dead bark.

Birdseye A distinct type of decorative figure on the tangential surface of timber caused by indentations in the cambium layer, particularly common in maple.

Board A piece of timber with wane on at least one of the edges.

Board foot A unit of measurement of timber equivalent in volume to a piece 12 inches (305mm) square and 1 inch (25mm) thick.

Bole A tree stem or trunk large enough for converting into boards.

Book match A way of jointing, where successive boards sliced from a log are turned over, like the pages of a book, and joined together.

Bound water The moisture in timber contained within the cell walls.

Bow A type of warp that produces a curve along the length of a board.

Burr An outgrowth on the side of a tree caused by a mass of small growing shoots. The resulting jumbled grain produces highly decorative figure when sliced.

Cambium The thin layer of actively growing cells between the bark and the wood which actively divides to produce new cells on either side.

Case hardening A drying defect that is caused by the outer layers of timber drying much quicker than the wet inner core. This results in permanent drying stresses.

Cell The basic building block of wood tissue consisting of a central cavity surrounded by an outer wall. Cell types include tracheids, vessels, fibres, parenchyma and rays.

Cellulose A carbohydrate which is a major constituent of wood cell walls.

Chainsaw mill An accessory fitted to a chainsaw that allows conversion of logs on site.

Checks A lengthwise separation of wood cells along the grain as a result of uneven shrinkage, commonly seen on end grain surfaces.

Close piling Stacking of freshly sawn boards without separating stickers.

Collapse The irregular surface of wood resulting from cell structure damage caused by incorrect drying.

Compression wood A type of reaction wood that forms on the underside of leaning branches of conifers.

Conditioning Exposing timber to a controlled relative humidity in order to achieve the required moisture content.

Conifer Trees of the genus gymnosperms characterized by needle-like leaves. These are usually evergreen trees.

Crotch Highly figured wood taken from the area where a branch joins the main trunk.

Cubic foot Unit of measurement of timber equivalent to a piece 12in x 12in x 12in (305mm x 305mm x 305mm).

Cup A type of warp where the board curves across the width.

Debarker A saw mill machine that removes the bark from a butt by grinding or chipping it off.

Deciduous A type of tree where the leaves fall off after the yearly growth cycle, typical of most hardwoods, but not all.

Density Weight of wood substance per unit volume.

Dicotyledons A class of plants within the angiosperms characterized by having two seed leaves. All hardwoods are dicots.

Diffuse porous Hardwood species when the vessels formed throughout the growth ring are of uniform size and distribution.

Drying defects Irregularities caused by incorrect drying procedures that damage or affect the strength and quality of the timber.

Earlywood A band of quick grown cells produced early on in the growing season and characterized by larger cells with lower density.

End checks A drying defect caused by the ends of the boards drying faster than the rest of the timber.

End sealing Coating the ends of boards to slow down the rate of drying to minimize end checking.

End grain The cross-sectional surface of a board.

Equilibrium moisture content The point at which moisture no longer enters or leaves a piece of wood at a given humidity and temperature.

Extractives Substances deposited in wood as it changes from sapwood to heartwood. These impart colour and resistance to decay.

FAS 'First and seconds' a top grade of hardwood timber that is at least 80 per cent defect free.

Fibre A specific hardwood cell type that contributes to the strength properties of timber.

Fibre saturation point The moisture content at which all the cell cavities are empty, but the cell walls are still saturated.

Fiddleback A type of figuring caused by wavy grain, commonly used in musical instruments.

Figure The distinctive pattern on the longitudinal wood surface caused by anatomical features, defects and the orientation of the log during cutting.

Free water Moisture contained in the cell cavities.

Grade A description of the quality of boards based on a recognized set of rules that take into account any of the defects.

Grain The direction of the wood fibres relative to the long axis of the tree trunk.

Green Freshly cut or unseasoned material with a moisture content above the fibre saturation point.

Gymnosperm The class of plants having bare seeds, including all softwoods.

Honeycombing Internal checks usually following the orientation of the rays, caused by case hardening due to incorrect kilning.

Hygroscopic Having the ability to absorb water.

Incipient decay Early stages of decay or rot where there may be some discolouration, but no loss of mechanical strength.

Isotropic Having the same properties in all directions.

Juvenile wood Wood formed around the central pith of the tree in the first few years of growth.

Kiln A chamber for drying timber under controlled moisture and temperature conditions.

Kiln-dried timber Material which has been dried in a kiln to a specified moisture content, usually well below what can be attained by air drying.

Knot A section of a twig or branch that has been overgrown by the expanding girth of the bole. Knots can be live or dead.

Latewood The section of the growth ring formed after the earlywood, usually containing smaller cells with thicker walls and a higher density.

Longitudinal Parallel to the main axis of the tree.

Lumen The empty space enclosed by the cell walls.

MDF Medium density fibreboard, a munufactured board made from compressed wood fibres mixed with resins.

Moisture content The weight of water in a piece of timber expressed as a percentage of the dry weight.

Moisture meter An electronic device used to give an instant readout of the moisture content.

Parenchyma Thin walled cells adapted for food storage and distribution.

Phloem Tissue making up the inner bark for conducting food throughout the tree.

Pith The small, soft and spongy core at the very centre of the tree. May be hollow in some species.

Pits Small sections of the cell wall that allow fluid to pass through into adjoining cells.

Plain sawn A way of cutting a log by slicing tangentially through the growth rings.

Plank A piece of timber with both edges square.

Quarter sawn Boards cut with the growth rings as near as possible at 90° to the face. This is used to reveal decorative figuring in species with heavy rays.

Ray Flat tissue bands orientated perpendicular to the trunk for transport of food materials across the stem.

Reaction wood Abnormal wood formed in leaning trees and branches. It's called compression wood in softwoods and tension wood in hardwoods.

Reclaimed wood Timber cut from previously used old beams and furniture.

Relative humidity Ratio of the amount of water actually present in the air relative to the amount it could theoretically hold.

Resin canals Areas in softwood tissues where resin is deposited as a protective measure, usually as a result of damage.

Rift sawn Wood that has been cut so the growth rings are at angle of between 30° and 60° to the face.

Ring porous Hardwood where the quick growing earlywood vessels are very much larger than the later grown vessels, resulting in a distinctive annual ring.

Sap Water in the tree containing dissolved food substances

Sapwood The active timber comprising of the most recent annual rings, it's usually lighter in colour than the heartwood.

Seasoning The lengthy process of drying wood to a usable state.

Shake A timber defect where the wood separates lengthwise. This often occurs along the growth rings as in a ring shake.

Shrinkage Changes in dimension that occur in wood as it dries below the fibre saturation point.

Softwood Wood from coniferous trees in the botanical group called gymnosperms.

Spalted Partially rotten wood that exhibits highly decorative colouration due to the fungal zone lines.

Specific gravity The ratio of the weight of a piece of wood relative to the weight of an equal volume of water.

Split Separation of the wood tissue that extends completely through a board, usually on the end.

Stickers Small pieces of wood normally about ¾in (19mm) square used to separate wet boards for drying.

Stripe A pattern resulting in timber where the grain direction is reversed in a regular sequence across the width. This is best highlighted by quarter sawing.

Surface checks Shallow cracks in the timber surface caused by uneven drying or exposure to heat.

Tension wood The reaction wood found in leaning stems of hardwood, always forms on the top.

Texture Describes the size of cells in the tissue make-up, ranging from very fine to coarse.

Tracheids Long conducting cells making up most of the tissue in softwoods. These are also found in a few hardwoods.

Trunk The main section of the tree producing the bulk of the timber.

Twist A type of warp where the corners move out of the same plane during drying.

Veneer Thin layers of timber cut by slicing or peeling, normally about $^1/_{32}$in (0.6mm) thick.

Vessels Large conductive cells with no end walls connected to form tubes in hardwoods.

Wane Bark left on the edge or the corner of a piece of timber.

Warp Distortion of the face or edge of the board away from the intended shape of the piece. This may take many forms such as bow, cup, twist or spring.

Xylem The portion of the tree inside the cambium, but excluding the pith.

Further reading

Wood Identification and Use
Terry Porter
GMC Publications
ISBN 978 1 86108 436 1

What wood is that?
A manual of wood identification
Herbert L. Edlin
Stobart and Son
ISBN 0 85442 008 8

Timber
Rik Middleton
Argus Books
ISBN 978 0 85242 955 6

Timber
Its structure, Properties
and Utilization
H.E. Desch
MacMillan Press
ISBN 978 0 33325 751 7

The Conversion and Seasoning
of Wood
William H Brown
Linden Publishing
ISBN 978 0 94193 614 9

Understanding Wood
A craftsman's guide to wood technology
R. Bruce Hoadley
Taunton Press
ISBN 978 091 880 405 1

Woodworkers Guide to Wood
Rick Peters
Sterling Publishing
ISBN 978 080 693 687 1

Woodturning Full circle
David Springett
GMC Publications
ISBN 978 1 86108 531 3

Turning Vintage Toys
Chris Reid
GMC Publications
ISBN 978 1 86108 602 0

Suppliers

Smee Timber Ltd.
Winsford Sawmills,
Smoke Hall Lane,
Winsford,
Cheshire.
CW7 3BL
01606 555500

Whitmores Timber
Main Road,
Claybrooke Magna,
Nr Lutterworth,
Leicestershire,
LE17 5AQ
01455 209121

Yandle and Sons Ltd.
Hurst Works,
Martock,
Somerset,
TA12 6JU
01935 822207

Record Power Ltd.
Unit B,
Ireland Industrial Estate,
Adelphi Way,
Staveley,
S43 3LS
0870 770 1888

Timberline
Unit 7,
Munday Industrial
Estate,
58-66 Morley Road,
Tonbridge,
Kent,
TN7 1RP
01732 355626

Lincolnshire Woodcraft Supplies
The Old Sawmill,
Burghley Park,
London Road,
Stamford,
Lincolnshire,
PE9 3JS
01780 757825

Alan Holtham has been involved in all aspects of woodworking for over 30 years. After graduating with a degree in Forestry and wood science, he established a specialist woodworking business supplying tools and machinery to customers all over the world, as well as importing and processing timber for both retail and wholesale customers.

After 20 years at the 'sharp end' of retailing, he decided to take a step back to concentrate on sharing his accumulated knowledge and experience. In 2000, Alan set up a dedicated film studio and workshop, initially producing instructional and promotional videos covering all aspects of woodworking machinery. The media business grew rapidly and Alan has now written hundreds of magazine articles and continues to write and present a variety of woodworking programmes on DVD.

He has also appeared on many TV woodworking programmes and regularly demonstrates tools and techniques on behalf of major machinery or tool manufacturers.

His simple, down-to-earth approach fronts a personal ambition to demystify woodworking and bring it back as a mainstream interest for everyone. Alan is passionate that woodworking should be particularly accessible for youngsters who are often neglected by an education system that does not prioritize teaching practical skills.

Index

To place an order, or to request a catalogue, contact:
GMC Publications Ltd.
Castle Place, 166 High Street, Lewes, East Sussex, BN7 1XU
United Kingdom
Tel: 01273 488005 Fax: 01273 402866
Website: www.gmcbooks.com
Orders by credit card are accepted